THE SWEATER CHOP SHOP

THE SWEATER
CHOP SHOP

Sewing One-of-a-Kind Creations from Recycled Sweaters

CRISPINA ffRENCH

Storey Publishing

The mission of Storey Publishing is to serve our customers by publishing practical information that encourages personal independence in harmony with the environment.

Edited by Deborah Balmuth and Kathy Brock
Art direction and book design by Alethea Morrison
Text production by Jennifer Jepson Smith

Cover illustrations by © Marguerite Sauvage, incorporating photographs by © Kevin Kennefick
Back cover and spine photographs by Mars Vilaubi
Interior photographs by © Kevin Kennefick, except for pages 6–7 (background), 10, 12, 16, 21, 28–32, 38, 42, 45, 47, 50, 56, 60, 64, 66, 76, 80, 87, 88, 94, 96, and 102 by Mars Vilaubi
Illustrations by © Crispina ffrench, except for pages 43, 47, 51, 57, 67, 77, 81, 84, 90, 103, and 107 by © Marguerite Sauvage, incorporating photographs by © Kevin Kennefick

Indexed by Mary McClintock

© 2009 by Crispina ffrench Swindlehurst

Printed in China by SNP Leefung Printers Limited
10 9 8 7 6 5 4 3 2 1

Library of Congress Cataloging-in-Publication Data

ffrench, Crispina.
    The sweater chop shop / by Crispina ffrench.
        p. cm.
    Includes index.
    ISBN 978-1-60342-155-3 (pbk. : alk. paper)
    1. Textile crafts. 2. Sweaters. 3. Clothing and dress—Remaking.
    4. Recycling (Waste, etc.) I. Title.
TT699.F465 2009
746—dc22
                                        2009013732

DEDICATION

To my son Ben, who grew up and
developed along with me and my technique, offering
support and sharing in the adventure.

CONT

ENTS

THE DINOSAUR RAGAMUFFIN,
see page 124

INTRODUCTION

In 1987, a felting artist named Layne Goldsmith presented her art to the fiber department at Massachusetts College of Art in Boston, where I was a student. We made felt. The cold, messy wetness of the process made it less than fun for me, yet, somehow, the texture of the finished product made the whole process seem worth it. The felt I created that day was later turned into the first Ragamuffin. The dinosauresque creation was stuffed with newspaper and moved like a marionette with loose appendage connections.

Shortly thereafter, I joined a juried craft-store cooperative in Cambridge, Massachusetts. Ragamuffins sold as fast as I could make them. Intensified by this unexpected demand for Ragamuffins, my lack of passion for the traditional felting process was limiting my ability to keep up with demand. Not only was the process wearing on my wrists, but the available colors of raw fleece were drab and mottled, not inspiring. One day while my dad and I were chatting about the bottleneck in my production process, he said, "Why don't you use shrunk wool sweaters from thrift stores for raw material?" It sort of just rolled off his creatively minded tongue without hesitation or, it seemed, much premeditation.

Soon, most outings incorporated escapades at thrift stores as I searched for knitted wool in great colors and patterns. As time went on, my need for sweaters surpassed my easily accessible supply. Bruce Cohen, the proprietor of Harbor Textiles/The Garment District in Cambridge, Massachusetts, became my first wholesale supplier. Soon I was buying 1,000-pound bales of wool sweaters, but the demand still outweighed my supply. I now had 40 employees, and all the products we sold were made from used sweaters. They were simple, using inexpensive tools and materials, and it was easy to teach untrained employees to make them. No one had ever seen anything like what we were producing. Our hand sewers and studio staff were alchemists, like Rumpelstiltskin, and I loved that.

So here it is, the knowledge I've gained on this wooly adventure. I share it with you, with the hope of inspiring empowerment, creative reuse, and environmental compassion.

♡ Crispin

CHAPTER 1

THE ARTFUL BEAUTY OF RECYCLING

WOOL SWEATERS

My concept of crafting — making functional art from recycled goods — has to do with making things that are super desirable, but with little material cost.

This translates, *in my head, to* SPINNING STRAW INTO GOLD.

Crafting from recycled goods is all about taking opportunities that are right in front of us to make (or do) something amazing, and being conscious that culturally discarded goods are just that — goods — and can be used to make beautiful things.

Discarded material offers more valuable feedstock than fresh, unused material. The energy, life force, and history of each person connected to an old sweater adds an enriching quality to each finished project, not found in new-material replicas.

The ease with which people are able to learn and accept the process of making things from recycled goods is another strong selling point. The tools needed for these projects are few, readily available, and affordable. The materials — used wool sweaters and yarn — are fairly inexpensive and abundant. Sweaters are commonly found in thrift shops, at garage sales, or in your family's closet, and nice sewing yarn is for sale at craft shops and online. The sewing stitches are quick and easy to learn, and they clearly display the handmade element. These aspects encourage people, regardless of their budget, to learn and experiment with the process.

THE CHALLENGES AND REWARDS OF RECYCLING SWEATERS

When working with wool sweaters to create new, more useful things, overlook undesirable characteristics of the garment, such as a regrettable style or state of shrunken-ness. These mishaps often become delightful details that can be used to successfully complete a project with just the right special feature. For example, a bright orange sweater might be too intense to appeal to most people, but a bright orange stuffed toy or a touch of orange as a detail on a Crispina sweater can be just great. A sweater that has shrunken too much to fit can be cut apart and used for pockets, blanket squares, a stuffed toy component, or layers of color in a wreath. An unfortunate stain or hole can be covered with decorative stitching or a felted appliqué that becomes an element of your design. When selecting sweaters, look at color, shape, knitted texture, softness, and fiber content. These characteristics will play a role in your finished work even more than the style, state of repair, or size of the original sweaters.

While it is my personal mission to make use of every last bit of material while staying committed to making super desirable, sought-after things, it is challenging and can become stagnating. Don't worry about how much material you are using or saving until you have had time to learn the process. If you are someone who is enthusiastically taken by the process, it is possible to use every scrap and have a "zero waste factor," but it is more important to have fun with the creativity, knowing that there are additional skills to develop if you so desire. Rather than using newly generated material that consumes energy to manufacture, creating art from recycled goods is a net gain: saving the consumption of new resources, reducing the need for landfill area, *and* offering a creative outlet to anyone interested.

GETTING STARTED

The first thing you will need to do is hunt for wool sweaters to cut up. Thrift shops and yard sales are good places to begin. This book could change the way you shop and the way you see used clothing. Thrift stores will become supply shops full of color and pattern and all manner of wild combinations of the two. Used sweaters become collections of components, of body and sleeve shapes, closure options, color or texture swatches, ideas, and inspiration.

Ask your friends and family if they have wool sweaters that are not useful to them anymore. If you are really jazzed about this kind of crafting, you can collect sweaters at your workplace or your kids' school. Be creative; people love to recycle and are normally pretty happy to contribute. The gift of a "wedding blanket" is even more meaningful when made from sweaters of family members. Send your kid off to college with a patched blanket made from their outgrown childhood sweaters and maybe a few of your own, or their sibling's, or granny's. It is fun to make things from sweaters with special memories, or from those you have received from friends or family members; however, it is important to be selective about fiber content. As you will read later, go for wool. Find the freedom to play with color, texture, and pattern. There is no wrong way to combine the aesthetics of the material. It is completely up to you.

I think the hardest part of making art with recycled goods, no matter what the material, is the cutting process. Cutting cloth accurately is not easy for many people. It is best if you can begin with nice flat sweaters and cutting simple, straight-edged shapes, like squares, with a rotary cutter. Chapter 3 is all about how to create a few different things using squares. Pot holders make an easy and fun beginner project, a very simple yet useful item for your first practice lesson. This will introduce you to the tools and the process with small, easily handheld work that can be simple or intricate, depending on the maker's desire and skill level. Follow the pot holder project by making a scarf; you can continue to become familiar with the cutting process and practice and experiment with different stitches, colors, and pattern combinations.

Once you have practiced the stitches and handled the material in those two projects, jumping around to the more involved projects is up to you. Cautious learners can follow the order established by the book, adding expertise as you go and reaching the end with a wealth of new skills and finished projects. As you get involved with the process, you will develop new techniques of construction or use passed-down sewing tricks that apply.

Share your knowledge, trade it around, learn how other people do things, and use what makes sense as your own. Use this teaching book to create community or to further develop your established one. Start a "project-of-the-month club" where everyone meets with their cut material to share the colors, patterns, and textures they have found with the others; then go home and make the project, meeting again in a month to compare notes, share tricks, and start the next project. All the while, beginners can get help from a buddy, and experienced sewers can share their knowledge.

Whether you take this medium on alone or as part of a group, satisfaction is gained in the experience. Project completion, friendship/connection, recycling/environmentalism, learning/teaching, and community building are all by-products of the process I have developed and teach here. My hope is that you find it appealing enough to develop even further with your own personal style.

CHAPTER 2

ASSEMBLING YOUR MATERIALS AND CHOP SHOP TOOLBOX

I LOVE WOOL.

Wool is processed fleece, or hair, of sheep. Humankind has been using wool to create textiles for thousands of years as part of an agricultural biosystem. Sheep provide raw material for textiles, milk, meat, lanolin, and land maintenance. Fleece is shorn from the sheep, usually annually, and processed by cleaning, carding, and typically, spinning into yarn that is then used to knit or weave cloth. Sheep fleece, along with llama, alpaca, and goat hair, has a unique characteristic enabling cloth made from it to felt, or mat together. Each hair fiber has microscopic "hooks" that, when agitated in hot water, become entangled and create felt.

Types of wool vary in their readiness to felt. It is a process that continues with ongoing agitation until a hard and very dense texture is achieved. People all over the world have discovered and taken advantage of this quality: Nomadic people of Central Asia build their houses of felt, and Arctic Russians wear boots that are made from only a thick layer of felt. Felt, and wool in general, keeps you warm even when it is wet, repels water, and is lightweight. Wool holds dye like no other cloth, with flagrant luminescence and richness of tone. Wool is soft and gentle on cutting blades, preserving sharpened edges without much need for upkeep.

While all of these things are true, and reason enough for me to love the stuff, I have seen great changes in the amount of wool we use in our culture. I think this is a result of the introduction of Polar Fleece — a synthetic cloth typically made of polyester. While Polar Fleece does not shrink or itch like wool can, it does pill when washed and harbors more static electricity than any other fiber I have used. Some Polar Fleece is made from recycled plastic bottles, but most is not. Wool is all made from animal fleece, grown in nature, supporting an agricultural biosystem with a long history.

WHAT TO LOOK FOR IN OLD SWEATERS

When selecting sweaters for crafting it is important that the knit is standard gauge "sweater knit" — the stitches should not be too big or too small — and the fiber is at least 70 percent wool (or other animal fibers including alpaca, angora, cashmere, and mohair). It is fine to use sweaters that have been shrunk already, or that have holes or stains. Here are some other cautionary guidelines in selecting sweaters that will yield the best felt:

* *Do not use sweaters made from superwash wool. Superwash wool has been treated with chemicals to keep it from shrinking or felting.*
* *Avoid sweaters made with more than 30 percent synthetic fibers such as acrylic, nylon, Dacron, polyester, Orlon, and polyimide or nonanimal derived natural fibers such as cotton, silk, ramie, or linen. Always check the label, and be wary of sweaters that don't have one.*
* *Do not use crocheted or open-knit wools.*
* *Avoid both ends of the knitted-gauge spectrum: neither extra-fine wool jersey (such as T-shirt-weight knitted wool) nor heavy double-knit, ski-style sweaters are good beginner choices.*
* *Do not try to felt tiny baby or doll sweaters as the yield is minimal.*
* *Avoid woven wools, which do not felt as well as knitted wool and unravel when cut.*
* *Do not use wool that is not soft, or any colors, textures, or patterns that you don't like.*

Pullovers have the biggest expanses of useful material, but cardigans and vests are also useful for most projects. When gathering material, get more than you think you will need. If the project calls for six garments, gather more. Many of the projects taught here are most successful when made with material of similar weight. It is nice to have the ability to be selective, as felting often has unexpected results that make it hard to know what sweaters will work well together before they have been processed (see page 20). Having abundance also allows for design choices as you work.

Inevitably you will find yourself with some sweaters that did not acquire the desired texture. After felting you may find that some of the sweaters fall into the "not so useful" category for your first project, but there is a place to use every sort of wool knit you could possibly come across. Even

working with this medium as long as I have, it's often hard to know this ahead of time, but once you have them, there usually are places they can be used. Big knobby hand- or open-knit sweaters that don't shrink to a nice felty texture can be used in Bobbles (see page 170) or the Home-for-the-Holidays Wreath (see page 164), even if they are likely to unravel easily with handling. So if you are excited to learn the whole process, hold onto all the material you do not use, both scrap and sweaters you sorted out.

the differences between knit wool and woven wool

There are two different types of fabric structure used in making wool garments. The majority are knits, which are stretchy even without spandex. This structure is made with one continuous thread or yarn that is knitted, the same way your granny might knit. (Knitted patterns are often created with additional colors and therefore more than one strand of yarn.) Sweaters, socks, and T-shirts are normally machine-knitted. Commercially made knitted garments are usually cut and sewn rather than knitted to a particular shape.

The second fabric structure, used in making garments other than sweaters, is woven. Woven cloth is

generally not stretchy, although with the introduction of spandex, woven textiles can have some stretch. Woven cloth is made with warp and weft threads in horizontal and vertical rows. The warp and weft can be different types of fiber. Jeans, corduroys, oxford cloth, and dress jackets are examples of garments usually made from woven cloth.

Wool sweater knits have many endearing qualities. They felt more easily than woven wools. They stretch and forgive nicely, and, when processed and felted as described, they do not unravel. Be sure that all the source materials you select for your projects are knitted, not woven.

Suitable Fibers

Wool, alpaca, mohair, angora, and cashmere are all animal-derived natural-fiber fabrics suitable for the projects herein. Select sweaters that contain as much of these fibers as possible, at least 70 percent. For some of my projects, as noted in the instructions, you're more likely to have success with a firmer felted fabric. For these, 100 percent wool might be in order.

After processing sweaters and woolen goods for more than 20 years, I've learned a lot about fiber, felting, and what works and what doesn't. These are some other things I have discovered:

* *Merino wool felts quickly and evenly. If you don't want a dense fabric, wash and rinse in warm water on a short cycle.*
* *Shetland wool does not felt as fast as merino wool, but is has a lovely texture when washed as described on page 20.*
* *Rag wool is not easy to felt and usually does not acquire a workable texture. It is recycled from other wool and, therefore, has already been through processing procedures, which may include hot-water dyeing and carding.*
* *Lambs wool felts like a dream but can become too dense if you are not careful while felting.*
* *Natural wool, which has never been dyed and exposed to hot water, tends to felt more quickly than dyed colors.*
* *Patterned knits often become very thick and too dense while processing. If you want to prevent that, wash in a short cycle with warm water.*

The best way to tell what will work most effectively is to process all your material, using the steps described on page 20, and see the results *before* deciding on your project. It is likely that you will have a project in mind before gathering your raw materials. You will find with experience, however, that not all sweaters create lovely felt. So before you get your heart set on using a particular sweater for a project, see how it felts first. It is a good idea to gather a few more sweaters than you think you will need to be sure that you are able to create enough felt with the desired texture.

PREPARING YOUR SWEATERS FOR A NEW LIFE

The soft, spongy texture created by washing and drying wool sweaters is very useful and easy to work with. The edges are stable and will not unravel, making construction a breeze for the beginner. It is easy to cut with scissors or a rotary cutter and it can be made in all sorts of cool colors and patterns. Wool sweater felt is warm, water resistant, and even fire resistant. (Wool is actually self-extinguishing, meaning that if you ignite a piece of wool cloth, it will burn for a second or two and then go out.)

Step 1: Processing

Before beginning any of the projects in this book, you must felt the sweaters you've selected. This requires three conditions — heat, moisture, and friction — which can be provided by your home washing machine and dryer. Here are a few tips for successful felting.

* *Use a hot-water wash, a cold-water rinse, and the usual amount (per load) of whatever laundry soap you have on hand.*
* *Set your home washing machine for the load setting that will allow free movement of your goods, but don't use too much water or they will float at the top and not get enough agitation or friction. If you desire a thicker, more shrunken finish, wash the sweaters in a load with your regular laundry. The weight of jeans and towels agitates the wool and enhances the felting process.*
* *Dry the sweaters in the dryer on high heat; this step tightens the felt further, and sometimes makes felt that lacks body become full of it!*
* *If, after one cycle of washing and drying, you still haven't achieved the desired felted texture, try repeating the process once or twice more.*
* *When your sweaters have felted enough to hold a crisp edge when cut, remove them promptly from the dryer, smooth them out, and stack them flat to store until you're ready to use them. This keeps the wrinkles at bay and the need for ironing to a minimum. It also allows for maximum visibility of your material palette.*

Even with the most complete and detailed instructions, it must be said that felting is an inexact science. The very nature of felting is unpredictable, and two sweaters with the same fiber content may give two very different results. I stress that you must check your sweaters frequently during the felting process, or you may discover your wool has shrunk too much and too densely. And once an item has crossed that line, there is nothing you can do. Felting is an irreversible, finite process. (But remember that no matter what the final result of your felting is, there is a use for it somewhere.)

If you have a sweater that is already felted (shrunk) that you would like to use in a project, you can clean it by washing on delicate (and a short agitation cycle), with warm wash and warm rinse; dry flat or in a cool dryer.

on desired texture

To determine if your felted sweater has the desired texture, make a test snip by removing the bottom edge of a cuff. Tug and stretch the cut edge a bit, then check for unraveling. It is fine if the cut edge holds the stretch, meaning if the tugging and stretching made that edge longer; it is not fine if you see a strand of yarn pulling away from the cut edge or little loops of yarn coming to the surface of the cut edge.

Keep in mind that felting happens at different rates; differently felted textures are useful for different things. Most people think of felt as a solid surfaced, stiff fabric. Stiff cloth is certainly useful for some projects, but soft, pliable cloth is usually your goal and is easier to use. As long as the edge is crisp and holds when cut, the sweater is suitable for use in these projects.

crisp edges — wool has desired texture

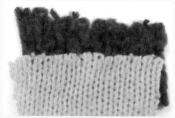

ravely edges — wool requires additional felting

Step 2: Sorting

Once you have decided on a project to make and washed and dried your sweaters, sort through them and divide into two piles: one for cloth that has acquired the desired texture and is ready to use, the other for sweaters that are not suitable for your purposes.

the results are only as good as the ingredients

Once you've washed and felted the sweaters you've collected, it's important to be critical about the results. The suitability of the processed material for the project makes the project beautiful — or not. Be sure to consider this step carefully before you begin cutting and investing energy in constructing your project.

THE RE-CONSTRUCTION PROCESS

Before you begin to cut out the pieces for your new project, you will probably want to iron some, if not all, of the sweaters you have washed. Use the lowest heat/steam setting on your iron. It is much easier to cut a nice flat fabric. If you have stubborn creases or wrinkles, lay the sweater on your ironing board, cover the creased area with a wet washcloth, and place your iron on top of the cloth and hold for a minute or two to steam out the wrinkles.

Step 3: Layout and Cutting

If you're a beginner, I encourage you to make pattern pieces before cutting your fabric. Cereal boxes work well for patterns because they are free, readily available, and a nice, heavy weight, making it easy to trace around. (Not to mention that you are recycling!) Often I will design my pattern pieces first by drawing the general shapes I want on paper and then tweaking them before I make the final cardboard versions and cut them out with household scissors.

Once the pattern pieces are laid out economically on the felted fabric (see below), I like to trace around each one with a permanent felt-tip marker. The marker will soak into the cloth, leaving a moist but quick-drying dark line. Just be careful not to transfer the ink to unwanted places; sometimes the ink stains the pattern piece and inadvertently ends up on the felted fabric. As you cut out the pieces, work just inside the line and be sure that the black line is completely cut off, trimming bits as needed.

For all of the shaped pieces, use your sharp fabric scissors to cut. When cutting squares, I find it quicker to cut with a rotary cutter and ruler, measuring as I go. Using a rotary cutter

getting the most from each sweater

It's important to be economical in the cutting process so that you get as many pieces out of each felted piece as possible. Here are a few tips for efficient cutting:

* *Begin cutting by placing your pattern pieces at the edge of your material.*
* *When making multiple components from the same sweater, place them next to each other, leaving the smallest spaces possible between them.*
* *It is fun to incorporate details from the sweaters in the finished project. Include a pocket in a square cut for a blanket or scarf you are making. Button up a felted cardigan and cut squares right across the placket, including it in the finished piece. Ribbing, cables, and even seams are also nice details to use. Details to avoid include zippers that have been cut, holes, and stains. If you find holes or stains on your finished project, there are ways to make them beautiful with a little creativity (see Decorative and Mending Stitches, page 33).*
* *Save all your scraps for projects that call for scrap material (see chapter 6, pages 112–144).*
* *There are several ways to open a sweater, making the most use of the knit area (see page 40).*

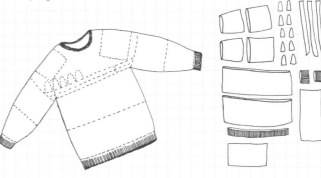

gives a clean, crisp, even edge. The difference between cutting with scissors and using a rotary cutter is like the difference between drawing a line with or without a straightedge. Not only is the rotary-cut edge free of nicks and wobbles, it is very easy to measure as you cut, reducing the time element while cutting.

When you've gained confidence in cutting, or if you're already experienced at it and feeling brave, you may want to try cutting freehand, or cutting shapes without patterns. With the exception of squares, I cut most everything freehand. For example, if I want to cut a circle big enough to use for a Ragamuffin head, my hand becomes my measuring tool. I place my hand (with fingers opened out) down on the fabric and cut around it, knowing that there needs to be about 1" of excess material all the way around the "circle" that is created by my flared fingers.

Another advantage of freehand cutting is it allows you to cut shapes that will fit on the fabric. Even if you need to cut a Dinosaur body and your pattern doesn't fit on the piece of cloth you have left, with freehand cutting you can make the needed Dino body longer and thinner, or shorter and rounder, to fit on the cloth. While freehand cutting can make the most efficient use of time and material, it is a skill that takes practice. If you are drawn to creating from felted wool, it is worth the time investment to master this technique.

Step 4: Sewing the Pieces Together

No prior sewing experience is required to make any of the projects in this book. They are all designed to be constructed by hand, without the use of a sewing machine. The stitching is done with large needles, often using yarn for thread. These are actually great projects for newbies to gain experience working with a thread and needle. In addition to felted sweaters and sewing yarn, just a few simple tools are required (see pages 24–25), making it possible to try these techniques without any major investment.

An additional perk to this way of crafting is its portability. You can cut out all the components you will need for your project, combine them into a kit, and take that kit on the road to do the sewing project along the way.

a word about sewing yarns

I like to use Persian wool for sewing together all the projects in this book. Persian wool is a 3-ply yarn with a somewhat loose twist most often used in stitching needlepoint. It is available in hundreds of colors, which is useful because, as you will soon see, yarn color can become a strong design element. Choose your yarn colors thoughtfully.

Persian wool is only a suggestion. You can substitute pearl yarn, tapestry wool, embroidery floss, or even sport- or worsted-weight knitting yarn, depending on the project and yarn availability.

THE CHOP SHOP TOOLBOX

Washing machine and dryer. It is very important to clean lint traps frequently when you are felting sweaters. All dryers and some washing machines have them. If you end up felting lots of sweaters, you might want to ask a plumber to install a simple lint trap for your washing machine outflow. Lint buildups can be the cause of a major headache (overflowing sinks) or a major expense (replacing burned-out dryers and blocked or clogged washers).

Ironing board and steam iron.

Two pairs of scissors. One sharp pair for cutting fabric; one pair of "household" scissors for yarn, cardboard, and everything else.

Sweater brush. This tool is very useful when you need to remove pills and other fuzz balls from the surface of a sweater. It looks like a small carding brush or cat brush, but it is softer and smaller and does the trick with ease. You just comb the surface of the material gently and the lint, pills, and other debris will come off in the bristles. If things get staticky, it's helpful to have a water mister on hand. You can find this handy brush at a yarn shop, fabric store, or online.

the point of fabric scissors

Sharp scissors make the cutting process super fun and a breeze. Dull scissors may make you change your mind about using this book!

I am very careful with my sacred fabric scissors and have been known to be a little "barky" to innocent borrowers in the studio. Good fabric scissors are expensive

and quite fragile. They hold a sharp edge well if used exclusively for cutting fabric. It is vital that they are not dropped on a hard surface. The slab floor in our studio has foiled many a pair by setting them off-kilter enough to render them dull. Professionally sharpen them as needed. I have found that caring well for fabric scissors, limiting the need for professional sharpening, is the best path to maintaining the sharpest tool.

Rotary cutter, extra blades, quilter's ruler, and cutting pad. Different size rotary cutters have different uses. For this work I prefer a 45 mm size.

Work gloves. I love my work gloves. They are deerskin, fit snuggly, and have molded to the shape of my hands. I can feel pretty well through them. They keep my fingertips from wearing out and allow me to hold an extra firm grip. When sewing, I usually wear a glove only on my right hand. (I am right-handed.)

Small spring-loaded pliers. Available at most hardware stores, pliers make some of the projects fun rather than painful. I like the smallest size, measuring nearly 5" from tip to handle end. They fit right in my hand and are easy to maneuver.

A 6' measuring tape. I like a soft measuring tape, retractable or not.

Ruler. Nice to have a 12" ruler handy for ease and maneuverability. (A T square may be useful for some projects.)

Pointy (but not "fine") black permanent felt-tip markers. Permanent markers dry faster, keeping the movement of the ink to a minimum. Pointy and not too fine are important because they tend to get caught in the knits you are drawing on.

Extra-long straight pins. Often called quilters' pins, the longer the better for pinning bulky fabric (1¾" are great).

Pincushion.

Needles

Yarn darner needles in sizes 14 to 18. These are sturdy, sharply pointed needles, 2½" to 3" long that are great for all-around hand sewing with the materials in these projects.

Doll needles. These are longer than yarn darners, 5" to 7" long, handy for sewing through extreme thicknesses of layered or stuffed components, such as Bobbles (see page 170).

Weaving needles. These are really heavy-duty, 5" long, with an eye that accommodates baling twine (see Home-for-the-Holidays Wreath, page 164).

Hand-sewing needles. For sewing with regular thread.

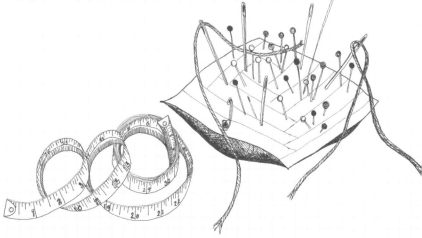

ORGANIZING YOUR WORK SPACE

A 4' × 8' table is an ample work space for the projects in this book. (I also use it, with padding, for ironing.) In my studio I have a table that is high enough to stand at while working, along with a tall stool. A lot of these projects can be done in a smaller space just as easily. Many people use floor space, but that is not comfortable for everyone. A typical kitchen table works. A card table would work in a pinch but might be a bit wobbly and too small for larger projects, especially sweaters and blankets. Small work spaces are fine if they are sturdy and you stay organized.

I use a simple leather tool belt I got at the hardware store to organize my hand tools and keep them at my fingertips. The many pockets hold everything I need. I wear it backwards, as suggested by my old studio neighbor and artful woodworker, Sanjiban, so the pockets are not as likely to empty themselves when I bend over. It is especially handy to keep the tools you use in the same pocket or pouch all the time so you always know where to find them.

It is important that your work space is comfortable and well lit. Make sure that the table height and chair-to-table height ratio is right for you. Set up a light source that is strong and clear, without an overtone of blue or pink. In addition to having a nice wall of windows in my studio, I have full-spectrum fluorescent light bulbs directly over my work space.

ironing your wool sweater material

Lots of steam works wonders with even the toughest creases and wobbles in creating a smooth, flat finish. (A "wobble" is a bump in a seam that is intended to lie flat against the surface fabric.)

If you need more steam than you are able to get by pushing the steam button, have a bucket of clean water and a terry cloth hand towel handy. Wet the towel and wring it out as much as you can; it should not be dripping wet. If you need to be able to see and manipulate the work, place the towel underneath it. If you just need a blast of steam to flatten and block something, place the towel on top of the work. The towel gets hot so use caution when moving it. (Work gloves might be in order.)

Let the iron float across the surface; it often is more effective to pick up the iron and place it down on top of especially bumpy bits. For bumpy seams, apply some steam to the surface. While the cloth is still hot and damp, manipulate the problem area with your hands to make seams straight, flat, and tidy; corners square; and edges even. Apply more steam and the weight of the iron for up to 60 seconds, fixing the manipulations in place.

BASIC STITCHERY

The general principle of pulling thread through cloth dates back 40,000 years to the first, primitive bone needles, since discovered in an archeological site called Kostenki in Russia. Needles close to those we know and use today were perfected in eleventh-century Spain. The basic stitches established centuries ago remain remarkably consistent. Here I've introduced a few simple stitches used in my projects to join layers of fabric together for durability and ease. While the names may vary, the techniques are ancient and something to honor and cherish.

THREADING NEEDLES

This is frequently the step that is most problematic for beginners, deeming the rest of their work frustrating and often fruitless. Use a needle that has a large enough eye to accommodate the yarn you are using. In your nondominant hand, hold the end of the yarn between your thumb and forefinger with just 1" sticking out. With sharp scissors snip the end blunt about ½" from your fingertip. Pick the needle up in your other hand and carefully wiggle the eye of the needle top to bottom over the cut end of the yarn. The tip of the yarn should come right through. Catch the yarn and pull it through. Knot one end of the yarn with either an overhand knot or a double overhand knot (see page 33).

EASING STITCHES OR SEAMS

This is the act of making something that doesn't really fit in a place, fit in that place. When you are asked to ease a stitch or a seam, you are being asked to sew two differently sized pieces of cloth together evenly. To make this work well, first pin the two pieces together by matching both ends of the seam you need to sew, then pin the middle together by measuring to the center of each piece, matching the two middles and pinning it in place. Continue on like this until you have pins every 2" to 3" and the fabric between them lies relatively flat.

GLOSSARY OF STITCHES

GLOSSARY OF STITCHES

RUNNING STITCH

The running stitch is quick and versatile. With just one pass of the needle you can catch many stitches by accordion folding fabric back and forth onto the needle before pulling through your length of yarn. This stitch is very functional, but it doesn't stretch well or protect cut edges.

To start, conceal the beginning knot

1. Knot end of yarn and insert needle under and up through the top layer of the finished piece.

2. Pull yarn through to sandwich knot between layers.

3. Secure the knot by poking your needle through the bottom layer and up through the top, wrapping the yarn around the outside edge (while holding the edges).

To sew

4. Hold the layers together, carefully guiding the overlapping edges even, or pin in place. Insert the needle in and out of the fabric being sure both pieces of material are caught with each stitch. Pull yarn all the way through, smoothing out the fabric to remove puckers and making sure the yarn is flush with the surface of the fabric.

5. End with needle coming through the back layer. Bring needle to the front, wrapping yarn around outside edges as at the start, and then poke through front to back to finish with yarn on back.

To finish

6. Tie a knot in yarn close to surface of the fabric.

7. Run needle back through several stitches to secure end and then snip off ¼" from the surface.

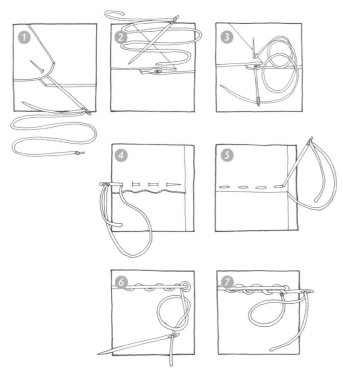

LADDER STITCH

This is time consuming since you can only make one stitch at a time. Ladder stitch is used on hems and where stretch is needed, like at cuffs or across stretchy spans of construction. The ladder stitch variation shown is used for joining butted edges.

To start, conceal the beginning knot

1. Knot end of yarn and insert needle under edge of top layer, coming up through the lower starting point for your first stitch.

2. Pull yarn through to sandwich knot between layers and begin your first stitch by poking needle down through adjoining single layer.

To sew

3. Work along entire span to be joined, poking needle down through single layer and back out through both layers.

To finish

4. After last stitch, poke needle through to the front; coming up under the joined edge, tie a knot close to the fabric surface.

5. To secure, poke the needle between layers for an inch or so. Snip off close to the surface of fabric.

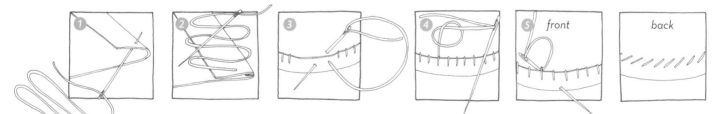

GLOSSARY OF STITCHES

GLOSSARY OF STITCHES

LADDER STITCH, VARIATION

This technique is useful for joining butted fabric edges and creating a seam that opens completely flat. A knitting needle (US size 3 or 4) is used to regulate stitch tension.

With right sides of fabric together, make an overhand knot in your yarn and pass the needle through the corner edges of both pieces of cloth. Pull through until knot is flush with the fabric. Wrap the yarn up over the knitting needle and into the fabric on the other side. Continue stitching, wrapping the yarn over the knitting needle for each stitch and always pushing needle in the same direction (either up from the bottom or down from the top).

right sides together

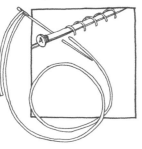

BLIND STITCH

When you want to join layers without a visible stitch, the blind stitch is an option. Working entirely on the inside of the two layers, try to catch just the smallest piece of fabric with each stitch so the stitches don't show through.

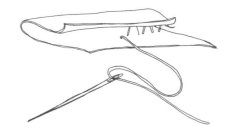

WHIP STITCH

Used to join "hold folds" in place or to join squares edge to edge, this quick, slanted stitch is less commonly used than the similar ladder stitch.

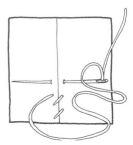

BLANKET STITCH

Used to finish edges and prevent unraveling, this stitch creates a running line of loops along the edge. It can also be used to join the edges of several layers.

1. Knot your yarn, poke the needle through from the wrong side to the right, then insert the needle back into the fabric in the same spot. Angle your needle up toward the edge to "catch" the loop of yarn and then pull through completely.

2. Insert the needle ¼"–⅜" away, at the same distance from the edge of your original stitch, angle the needle up toward the edge and catch the loop of yarn now extending along the edge from the last stitch.

3. When you come to a corner, make your last stitch at a distance from the edge equal to your stitch length.

4. Poke needle back through the same spot as beginning of last stitch and then continue down adjoining edge.

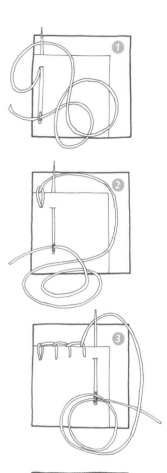

GLOSSARY OF STITCHES

GLOSSARY OF STITCHES

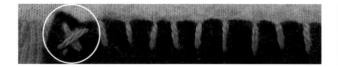

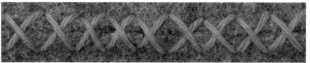

REINFORCED X STITCH

This stitch is used to reinforce stress points and to make bulky seams lie flat.

1. Complete the stitch just before the stress point or seam and bring needle back through the starting point.

2. Insert needle into fabric on other side of the stress point.

3. Make an X stitch crossing over the stress point, as shown.

4. Resume the regular stitch pattern.

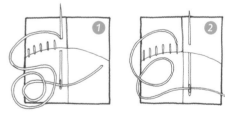

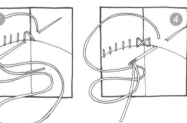

EDGE-TO-EDGE X STITCH

To work this stitch, used for joining butted edges, lay fabric flat on a work table with right sides up. (Alternatively, you can work with wrong sides of fabric together using the knitting needle technique detailed on page 30.) Note that two passes along the distance of the seam are required to complete the X.

1. Make a knot in yarn and insert needle into the back (wrong side) of one of the fabric pieces. Pull the yarn through and begin joining together the butted edges with a diagonal whip stitch (see page 30).

2. Finish your last stitch by bringing the needle out at the top of the stitch, close to the edge.

3. Reverse the direction of the whip stitch and traverse the seam in the opposite direction. For the most finished look, cross each X evenly on the way back by inserting your needle into the same holes created by the original stitches.

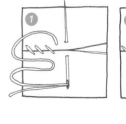

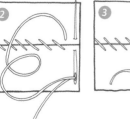

FINISHING KNOTS

These are used to secure the yarn when you finish a seam (or if you are running out of yarn). With needle still threaded, tie an overhand knot close to the surface of the cloth.

✳ OVERHAND KNOT

This is a sample knot used to stop your thread or yarn from pulling through.

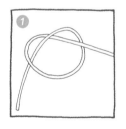 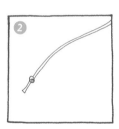

✳ DOUBLE OVERHAND KNOT

This is used when there is openness to the fabric, requiring a bulkier knot to keep the yarn from pulling through.

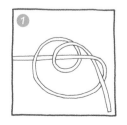

IN-PLACE OR DOUBLE STITCH

This term just means to go back over a stitch. It holds things in place, but not as securely as a knot.

DECORATIVE AND MENDING STITCHES

Although not essential to the construction process, there are some stitches that may prove to be helpful. They can be used as embellishment wherever you want or need, but they can also cover holes or stains that might show on your fabric. Even mishaps that happen after completion can be mended with any one of these.

BASKET WEAVE STITCH

STAR STITCH

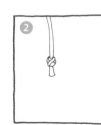

PATCH

GLOSSARY OF STITCHES

Basket Weave Stitch

Besides hiding spots or holes, this stitch looks nice on both sides.

1. Visualize a square or rectangle that encompasses all the area to be concealed with an ample margin.

2. Thread a tapestry needle with 1½ yards of thick, bulky wool yarn and make long vertical stitches across the square area. Cover the entire area.

3. Make a small diagonal stitch at lower end of corner.

4. Switch to a horizontal direction, weaving your needle over one strand and under the next until the area is completely covered.

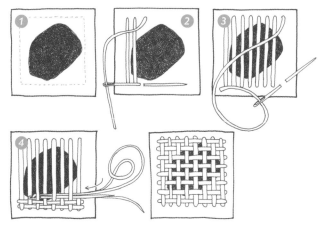

Single-sided Star Stitch

This stitch conceals small holes or stains.

1. Knot one end of your yarn and then poke the needle through the back of your fabric, coming out slightly above and to the left of the flaw you want to conceal.

2. Take a large diagonal stitch across the flaw. Poke the tip of your needle down into the fabric and then back up to the surface above.

3. Make a diagonal stitch in the opposite direction, creating an X. Poke the tip of the needle back to the surface directly below the flaw. Stitch across the flaw a third time to create a star.

4. To finish, knot yarn close to cloth on back and slide the needle under the other stitches before snipping off.

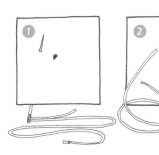
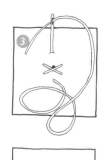

Double-sided Star Stitch

This stitch is a brilliant detail to add when mending small stains or holes on an item that will be visible on both sides, such as a blanket or scarf. This only works well on thick material.

1. Knot one end of your yarn. With the wrong side of fabric facing you, carefully slip the needle tip into a spot about 1" from the flaw. Direct it between the layers of fabric so the knot shows but the yarn is hidden in the thickness of the fabric.

2. Bring needle back to the surface in a spot above and to the left of the flaw. Knot yarn close to the surface, then poke needle through to the front side right next to the knot.

3. Make a long diagonal stitch across the flaw. Insert needle into fabric and then back up to your starting place, making sure the stitch looks nice on both sides.

4. Insert needle back into fabric at same spot and make a small sideways stitch hidden between layers.

5. Make a long vertical stitch across flaw, re-emerging at start of the stitch to form an X.

6. Repeat steps 4 and 5 to form star.

7. Knot yarn close to the surface and make a larger sideways stitch between the layers so needle tip emerges outside the star.

8. Snip off excess yarn at the surface. Snip off beginning knot.

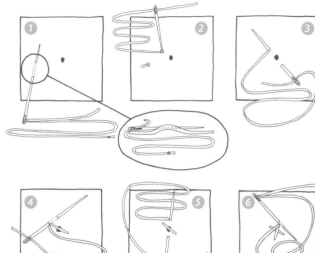

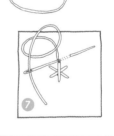

Patches

If you have a larger imperfection, a patch is the best solution. Thin, stable scraps of sweater material work best. If the edges are really crisp, you can leave as is. If your scraps are made of looser, softer cloth, press the edges under. To attach, ladder stitch around the whole circumference of the patch.

GLOSSARY OF STITCHES

CARING FOR YOUR FINISHED PROJECTS

All the projects described in this book are designed to last a good long while with care and normal use. The construction processes incorporate details that make the finished work durable, but not bulletproof. Ragamuffins are soft sculpture, not indestructible toys for roughhousing hell-raisers. Sweaters are designed to be worn in everyday life; snags in sewing yarns will happen, elbows might wear through. These and other mishaps can be repaired easily once you have learned the step-by-step processes spelled out in this book.

When cleaning is needed, gentle washing and laying flat to dry are the best ways to launder any of the projects taught in this book. You can follow these simple instructions to make that as easy as possible. (Before you get started, you might want to put on a short-sleeved shirt.)

1. Fill a washing machine with enough lukewarm water to allow the items you are washing to move freely. Add the recommended amount of laundry soap. Turn washing machine off.

2. Put in the items you would like to launder. Agitate gently with your hands, being careful not to wring or agitate fiercely as that can cause additional felting. Do not pull the wet item out of the water as it might be damaged by the weight of the wet material.

3. Set washing machine dial to spin cycle and turn it on. When spinning has stopped, turn the machine off.

4. Refill the washer with warm water and turn off. Gently agitate again, using your hands and arms to rinse out all the soap.

5. Set washing machine dial to spin cycle and turn on to remove excess water.

6. Remove laundered goods from washing machine, smooth out, and lay flat to dry.

If needed, use a dry iron on medium heat setting, before the item is completely dry, to remove any creases or seam wobbles. This works best while the item is still moist, eliminating the need for steam since it will be created by the moisture already present in the fabric.

If you are hand-washing an item without the luxury of a washing machine spin cycle, lay the freshly washed, clean item flat on a towel. (You can fold it to fit on a towel if necessary.) Roll up the towel and wet item together into a log shape, then roll the log shape into a ball. Apply as much pressure as you can, squeezing the water from the clean item into the towel. Unroll the towel and lay the item flat to dry completely.

CHAPTER 3

STARTING FROM SQUARE ONE

Projects made with squares are *fun for all and most* SUITABLE FOR BEGINNERS.

Cutting is clear, simple, and easy to do. Seams are straight, even, and short. If this is your first attempt at making something with felted wool, I recommend starting with the pot holder project to get your hands used to the work. Once you have completed a pot holder, a scarf would be a great next project to try, allowing experimentation with stitches and gaining experience with using several different fabrics.

As with all the projects, the texture of the felted sweaters you choose is very important. To make a beautiful finished piece, it is best to start with beautiful materials of similar weight. Choose your materials carefully, considering the color, weight, and hand of each sweater (*hand* means the feel of the fabric, including characteristics of drape, softness, and weight), and how that correlates to the project you have in mind.

PREPARING YOUR SQUARES

After you've selected your sweaters and processed them to the desired texture (see *pages 20–21*), sort them into three piles, according to density and structure.

* *Pile One: Soft, yet tight and most densely felted pieces. These are the sturdiest ones, which are likely to hold a nice straight cut edge and are best reserved for blankets and pillows.*

* *Pile Two: Thinner, softer pieces that drape nicely. These you would want snuggled up under your chin and are perfect for scarves.*
* *Pile Three: Whatever else is left that doesn't rate for either Pile One or Two. Thinner pieces can be layered to make pot holders, and pieces that are raveling or have holes or stains can be sandwiched in between as filler (if you are as obsessive-compulsive about recycling as I am!).*

As you start to imagine, there are many ways to make the materials you have work for whatever you want to make.

using patterns

Because I have been cutting items from felted wool for more than 20 years, I often do it freehand. But when cutting pieces like these squares, which need to look like squares and be the same size, I use a rotary cutter or a pattern. Flattened cereal boxes are my first choice for making patterns because they are free and almost everyone can get their hands on some; they are easy both to cut out and to trace around. So if you do not have a rotary cutter, save yourself some time and money and make a pattern.

To make a pattern that can be used for any project in this chapter, simply draw a 7" square onto the cardboard and cut it out. Using a permanent felt-tip marker, trace around the pattern onto the felted fabric. Cut out the squares just inside the marker line; this way the line will not be visible on your finished project.

OPENING SWEATERS

* BEGINNING (FOR ALL STYLES)

Carefully remove any tight ribbing at the cuffs and waist edges with scissors.

* PULLOVER

Cut open from sleeve end to hem on both sides.

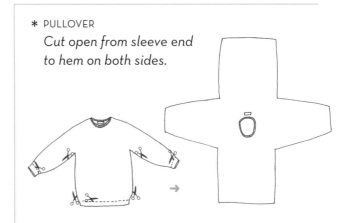

* CARDIGAN

If you want to incorporate the closure into the finished piece, cut from sleeve end to hem on both sides.

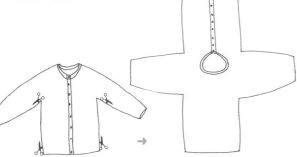

* CARDIGAN, VARIATION

If you do not plan to use the cardigan closure as a detail in your project, begin cutting from the neck edge along both shoulders and continue down along the top sleeve creases to the cuff edges.

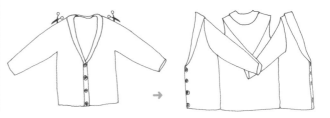

* VEST WITH FRONT OPENING

Cut open along both shoulder seams.

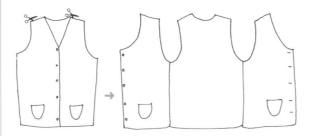

* PULLOVER VEST

Cut open along one side seam and across both shoulders.

Opening the Felted Sweater

Opening sweaters for cutting squares is an important part of the process that is the same no matter which project you are working on. The reason you open sweaters before you cut from them is so that you can clearly examine what you are working with, cutting around stains and holes and incorporating any details you like.

Before you open any sweater, carefully remove any tight ribbing at the cuffs and waist edges with scissors. The next steps vary depending on the sweater style.

* *Pullover sweaters are most useful cut open from sleeve end to hem on both sides. Begin cutting at either end and watchfully follow the existing seam. Once you have the sweater open, go back and cut carefully next to the seam to remove it completely.*
* *Cardigans can be cut this way, too, if you want to incorporate the closure into your finished piece. Buttons usually work well in this case; zippers do not because they don't shrink (they are almost always washable fabric, not wool), causing ripples in the fabric. Also, if you cut into a zipper, it no longer will zip and instead is liable to become an open hole in your work.*
* *For cardigans where you do not plan to use the closure as a project detail, you can open the sweater beginning at the shoulders and cutting along the top crease to the cuff edge. This will not give you a flattened piece, but it will produce the most useful expanses of cuttable cloth.*

* *Pullover vests can be opened along both side seams, or up one side seam and across both shoulders.*

Once you have opened the sweaters you will be using, press them with an extra steamy iron set to the "wool" (medium heat) setting. If your iron is not particularly steamy and you are battling creases and folds, try ironing with a wet dish towel on top of the sweater.

Size Guidelines

For the projects in this chapter, I recommend cutting all squares to the same size. The shape I most commonly use is a 7" square. It is an efficient size for cutting, yielding an average of seven or eight squares from each adult-size felted garment. Once you have the general gist of how these items are constructed, it is fun to work with many different size squares as well as incorporating rectangles of every proportion into the mix. However, be sure to consider the amount of time you have to make the item. The smaller the pieces, the more cutting and sewing time will be needed for completion.

As well as sticking to a standard-size square, the projects in this chapter use simple stitches to connect pieces for scarves and blankets. Freely embellish your work by using the more decorative joining stitches described in the Glossary of Stitches (see pages 27–35).

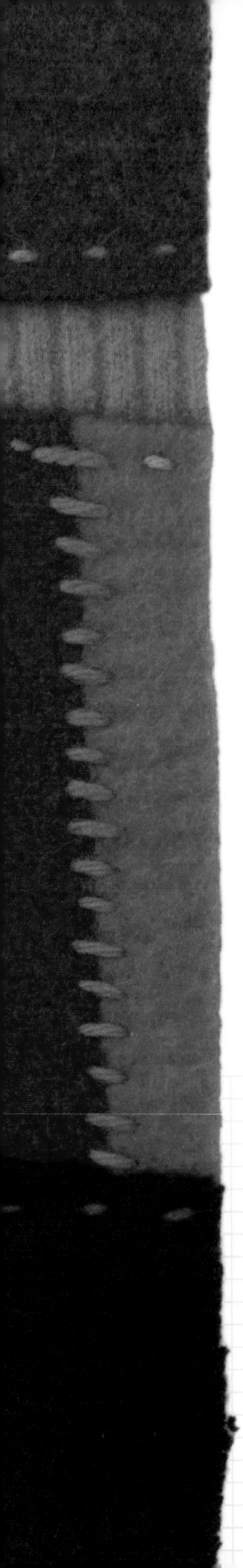

TIME REQUIRED **45 TO 60 MINUTES**

CUTIE-PIE POT HOLDERS

Pot holders may sound a little hokey — like something you might have brought home from summer day camp. I like "hokey" and find pot holders useful every day. They can really add a bright, inexpensive handmade spark to a kitchen. Making pot holders is quick and simple, and they are a great gift any time of year. Plus, because these are constructed with wool, they are fire retardant and insulating, making them super functional yet cute (of course).

The simplest design is to use a single 7" × 7" square top (see page 45). Once you've learned the basic technique, try patching pieces together to make colorful tops, such as the ones pictured at right.

you will need

- » Felted wool sweater (see page 20)
- » Sharp fabric scissors
- » Rotary cutter, pad, and extra blades *or* a 7" × 7" pattern made from cardboard (see Using Patterns, page 39)
- » Permanent felt-tip marker
- » One 7" square of woven cotton cloth for backing (an interesting patterned cloth is nice)
- » One 1" × 6" strip of nonraveling cotton jersey (such as T-shirt material)
- » Extra-long straight pins
- » A size 16 yarn darner needle
- » Persian wool or embroidery floss

CRISPINA'S
DESIGN NOTES

Fun fabrics for the backing of your pot holders are often easily found either around the house — look through your old clothes, tablecloths, or other items no longer being used — or at the thrift shop. Any type of garment will work as long as the fabric is not polyester or another synthetic that is prone to melting with prolonged heat exposure. Just look for a pattern or palette you like.

PREPARING YOUR MATERIALS

1. For each pot holder, carefully cut a 7" × 7" square from both the felted sweater and the woven cotton material you have selected. If the felt is thin, cut two or three squares to increase the thickness. (If you have traced around a cardboard pattern with a marker, be sure to cut just inside the line so no marker shows on the square itself.)

2. Place the wool and cotton squares wrong sides together with the cotton on top. If you are using more than one wool square, stack them together, carefully matching edges, and then add the cotton square to the top of the pile, right side up.

3. To make a loop for hanging the pot holder, fold the 1" × 6" rectangle of cotton jersey in half, short ends together. Insert 1½" of the two short ends in one corner between stacked layers.

4. Pin all four corners in place, being certain that you have "caught" both ends of the hanging loop.

SEWING

5. Thread your needle with a 2-yard length of Persian wool or embroidery floss. Beginning at the corner with the hanging loop, insert your needle under the cotton top layer and push down through the hanger and the wool bottom layer(s) of fabric. Pull yarn through to the bottom of the pot holder, concealing the knot under the top cotton layer.

STEP 5

6. Make a reinforced X stitch (see page 32) through the hanger and all layers in that corner. Stitches should be neat and strong and can show on both sides of the pot holder. This stitch will anchor the hanger and keep the layers in place; it also allows pin removal in this corner, making it easier to hold and work on the next steps.

7. Finish your X stitch with thread coming out of the fabric about ½" in from the cut edges of the layers, and begin to blanket stitch (see page 31) around the edges of the pot holder. Be sure you are catching all the layers with each stitch. Keep your corners neat and square by double stitching the first and last stitches of each side seam.

STEP 7

8. When you get back to where you started, tie an overhand knot close to the surface of the material. Run the needle and yarn between the layers about 1" to conceal it. Snip the yarn off at the surface of the pot holder.

9. Iron the finished pot holder with lots of steam to make a nice flat finish.

from single-fabric to patched tops

Once you've mastered the single-square pot holder tops pictured at right, you can create a playful look by patching together a variety of fabrics. Begin with four squares all cut to the same size. Cut one of the squares into four shapes of your choosing. Use these pieces as patterns to cut the other squares into the same shapes. Now mix-and-match the shaped pieces like a puzzle to form four complete squares. Join the pieces together with either ladder stitch variation or edge-to-edge X stitch (see page 32) to make a new set of four pot holder tops. Complete the pot holder project, beginning with step 2 on page 44.

TIME REQUIRED **1 TO 2 HOURS**

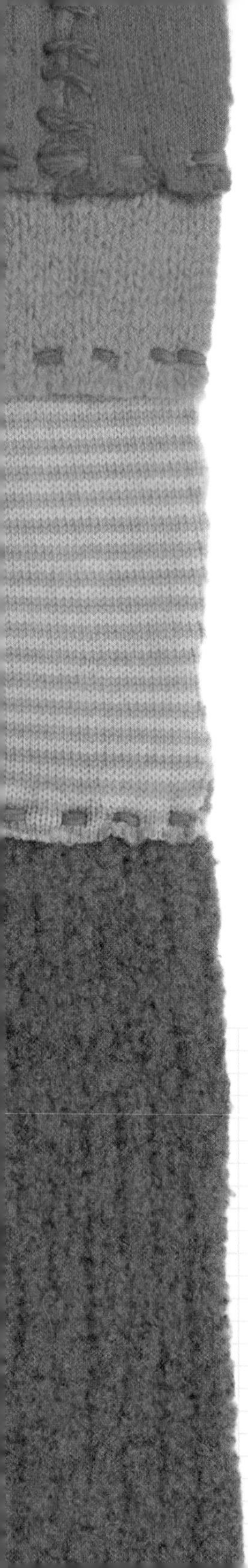

NECK NUZZLE MUFFLER

Scarves are simple and easy to make and can take on many different looks, depending on your material choices. Monochromatic scarves are subtle and more understated than ones with wild color and pattern combinations. A welcomed richness comes into play when combining many different felted fabrics into one finished piece. The fabrics used could all be of a particular color or hue, they could be all completely different in color or pattern, or a subtle combination with one or two contrasting squares to make a pop, producing several notably different style accessories.

you will need

- *Soft* felted wool sweaters in your choice of colors and textures (I like to make each square a different color, so you would need 12 sweaters)
- Sharp fabric scissors
- Rotary cutter, pad, and extra blades *or* a 7" × 7" pattern made from cardboard (see Using Patterns, page 39)
- Permanent felt-tip marker
- Extra-long straight pins
- Several colors of Persian wool or embroidery floss
- A size 16 yarn darner needle

STEP 1

PREPARING YOUR MATERIALS

1. Cut out twelve 7" squares using a rotary cutter and pad, or cardboard pattern, marker, and fabric scissors.

2. Pin the squares together, end to end, with a ½" overlap.

3. Separate the plies of your sewing yarn. Use three of the six strands of embroidery floss, or one or two of the three strands of Persian wool. Thread your needle.

SEWING

STEP 4

4. With a simple running stitch, sew the squares together. Be sure you catch both pieces with each stitch and be sure you are not sewing so close to the cut edge that the stitches will pull out. You can choose to conceal the knots or use them as a decorative accent.

5. Once you have the squares sewn together, you can add fringe, or other decorative variations or you can just leave the edges plain.

6. Steam iron the completed scarf, being sure to add extra steam at the seams to make a nice flat finish.

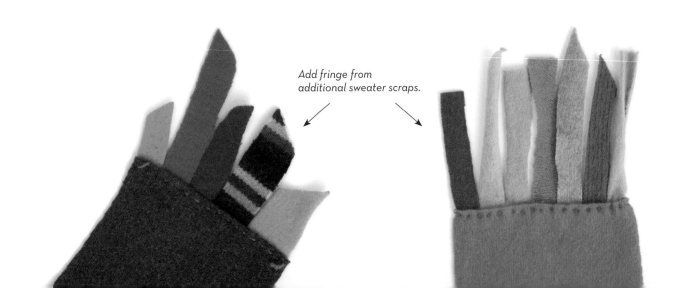

Add fringe from additional sweater scraps.

SCARF VARIATIONS

» *Sewing yarn color plays a key role.* Consider making a neutral-colored scarf stitched with hot pink or bright orange yarn — or both. Your material choices are key to making this something that will be worn and appreciated — go for soft and yummy material.

» *Incorporate pockets, buttons, plackets, and patches* to add an element of obvious reuse.

» *Add fringe* to either end by simply cutting seven or eight evenly dispersed 4" snips parallel to each other at each end square.

» *Add multi-colored fringe* by attaching skinny rectangular bits of scrap across each short end of the scarf with a running stitch.

» *Leave the yarn ends long* and the knots exposed at the end of your running stitches for a little fringe along the sides of the scarf.

Opt for no fringe at all.

Leave the yarn ends long for extra fringe at the sides.

Snip fringe from each end square.

SIMPLE PILLOWS

Because pillows are smaller than blankets, they are a good size project to try before taking on the larger item. We will begin with a simple version, but keep in mind that it is easy to change many characteristics of this project.

Consider your material options and have a general design in mind before you get started. While this is a great beginner's project, it is one that works great with scrap material. Unlike other projects, the material for pillows does not need to be consistent in density and "feltedness." Just be careful about using open knits as the pillow form may show through.

you will need

» 3 or 4 felted wool sweaters (see page 20)

» Sharp fabric scissors

» Rotary cutter, pad, and extra blades *or a* 7" × 7" pattern made from cardboard (see Using Patterns, page 39)

» Permanent felt-tip marker

» Extra-long straight pins

» A size 18 yarn darner needle

» Persian wool or comparable wool sewing yarn

» A 20" square pillow form

CRISPINA'S
DESIGN NOTES

If you're a beginner, you can use this project to gain familiarity with the process and not worry about details. If you're a more experienced sewer, you might have fun getting super detailed by adding embellishment and handwork, as shown in the pillow above.

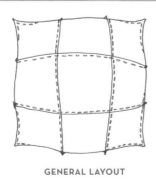

GENERAL LAYOUT

PLANNING YOUR PILLOW SIZE AND LOOK

First establish the size of the pillow you would like to make by finding a pillow form, sometimes called a pillow insert. You can create a cover for a premade pillow form; standard-sized pillow forms are readily available at craft and fabric stores. (The project that follows uses a 20" pillow form.) I often use a worn-out or outdated pillow for a base, removing the cover or just covering the unsightly one. (I'm always looking for ways to recycle.) You also can make your own pillow form in any size or shape you would like. Stuffing can range from raw wool or fleece (sheep hair) to finely cut scrap material, or even buckwheat, flax seeds, or balsam.

Next, decide whether you want to have wool on both sides of the pillow, or if you would like to back it with some other material that will be softer under your head (if it is that sort of pillow). Do you want to be able to open the pillow cover and remove the insert for cleaning? Think about what sort of closure you would like if you do think it should open. Finally, consider the fabric you will use. Most sweaters are big enough to nearly or completely cover an average-sized decorative pillow. Be sure to make your pillow cover interesting enough to warrant cutting up the sweaters you have gathered.

PREPARING YOUR MATERIALS

1. Cut out eighteen 7" squares using a rotary cutter and pad, or fabric scissors, a cardboard pattern, and a marker.

2. Arrange the squares into six strips of three squares each. Working one strip at a time, pin the connecting edges of the three squares with wrong sides together.

SEWING

3. Thread your needle and, with a simple running stitch, sew the squares in each strip together using a ⅝" seam on the right side of the fabric. Be sure to conceal your beginning and ending knots and match beginning and ending edges accurately.

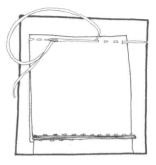

STEP 3

4. Sew three strips together, long edge to long edge, in the same way. You will have a square comprised of nine smaller squares; repeat with the remaining squares. You will have two nine-piece squares, each measuring approximately 18" × 18".

5. With wrong sides together, pin the 18" squares together on three sides, carefully matching the seams and corners.

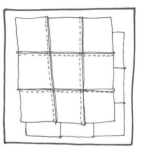

STEP 4

6. Using a running stitch, sew them together on the three pinned sides with a ⅝" seam. Carefully match seams front and back. Double stitch at each intersection, and double stitch at the corners as well.

7. Insert the pillow form, being attentive to corners. Push the insert down enough to pin the opening closed.

8. Sew running stitch across the opening to finish the pillow.

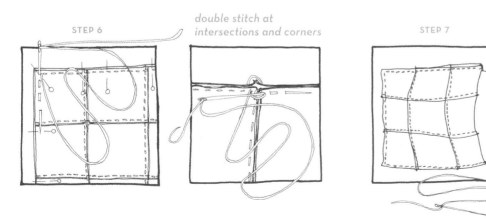

STEP 6   *double stitch at intersections and corners*   STEP 7

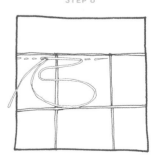

STEP 8

PILLOW VARIATIONS

While pillows are fun and relatively easy, they also offer a canvas to embellish with detailed handwork once you get going. There are all sorts of interesting things you can do to add to the intricacy of pillows. Here are a few ideas to get you thinking:

» *Try using alternative stuffing materials.* Balsam smells great and would make a lovely tiny pillow, while flax seed or buckwheat are sometimes used in horseshoe-shaped neck pillows, which can be heated in the microwave.

» *Add a closure.* Use snap tape, a zipper, hook and eye tape, buttons, or an overlap to allow your pillow to be opened and changed. (See pages 84–86 for details on using hook and eye tape, and pages 76–79 for inserting a zipper.)

Add a closure such as the snap tape shown below along one side.

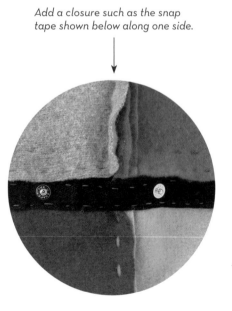

Appliqué parts of a beaded sweater or another decorative piece onto your pillow.

» *Get detailed* with embroidery, mixed stitches, appliqués, or smaller components sewn together.

» *Incorporate pockets, beaded sweater bits, and button plackets* from the sweaters you cut up.

» *Add decorations,* such as a flange, edging, buttons, or fringe.

Have fun and make beautiful stuff!

Incorporate a sweater pocket into one of the pillow squares.

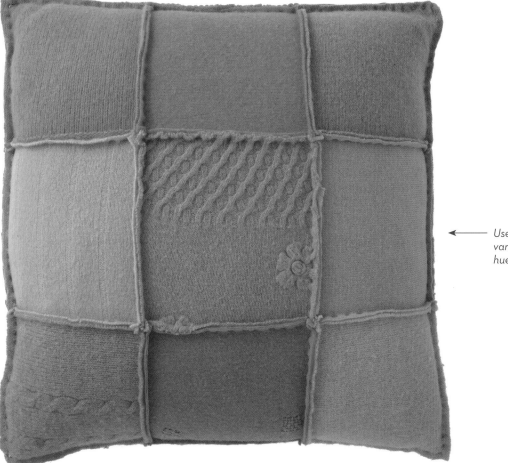

Use sweaters that are variations of the same hue.

KEEPSAKE BLANKETS

Blankets are my favorite thing to make because they are flat, open canvases, and they don't really wear out when made with quality in mind.

Before you get started, please read through this whole blanket project. With this knowledge, you will have an idea of what level of intricacy you would like to undertake before starting. Beginners might find it easiest to use all one-size components. My example shows how 7" squares work.

you will need

» About 8 felted wool sweaters (see page 20) for single-layer construction 5' × 5' throw; more or less as necessary

» Sharp fabric scissors

» Rotary cutter, pad, and extra blades *or* a 7" × 7" pattern made from cardboard (see Using Patterns, page 39)

» Permanent felt-tip marker

» Extra-long straight pins

» A size 18 yarn darner needle

» Several colors of Persian wool, embroidery floss, or other wool sewing yarn

optional

» Edging material of your choice in the following length (3" wide): 3¼ yards for stroller; 4½ yards for baby crib size; 5¾ yards for a throw; 8 yards for twin; 9¾ yards for double/queen; 10 yards for king

GATHERING AND SORTING YOUR MATERIALS

Blanket Layouts Using 7" Squares

STROLLER *(25 squares)*

CRIB *(42 squares)*

THROW *(64 squares)*

First, decide what size blanket you want. Figuring that the average sweater yields seven or eight 7" squares, gather a batch of felted wool sweaters (see page 20) that will make roughly twice the number of squares required for the blanket size you want to make. Only about a quarter of sweaters yield a felted fabric worthy of single-thickness blankets. To compensate for this shortcoming, you can simply double up the thin sweaters and add a design element by layering different colors; you also vastly increase the number of useful sweaters. You can use two squares from the same sweater or use two different squares that will make the front and back of the blanket different. (Be careful about doubling up sweaters that are not very thin and adding too much weight to your blanket).

Carefully sort the prepared sweaters into two or three piles according to density after processing (see page 21). Assess the materials you have gathered, considering the number of squares you will need to make the size blanket you would like. Do you have enough of a similar texture and density to make the blanket you are aiming for? What is the range of colors you would like to use? Do you need to add more?

When designing your blanket, keep in mind that it is essential to work with materials that are similar in density. If there is one sweater that

TWIN BED *(120 squares)*

DOUBLE/QUEEN BED *(144 squares)*

KING BED *(180 squares)*

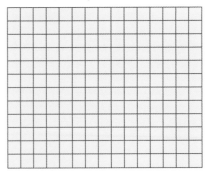

you really want to include that is much heavier than the others, be sure you arrange those squares evenly throughout the blanket. Most successful blankets are weighty and warm but soft enough to drape and feel snuggly. Larger blankets demand heavier-weight squares (this could mean more doubling) than smaller blankets to feel sturdy.

You can design your blanket layout by making a template similar to the diagram on the previous page (coloring in each square to see the end effect) or you can sew your components together randomly.

PREPARING YOUR MATERIALS

1. Cut out the number of 7" squares indicated on the diagram on the previous page — plus some extras if needed — for the size blanket you are making. (If you trace around a cardboard pattern with a marker, be sure to cut inside the line as you go.)

2. Either following a blanket design template, or randomly using cut squares, begin to organize your squares into rows. Gather all the needed squares for the first lengthwise row, stacking them in order if you're using a template, or randomly if that's your desired effect. In order to save work space, stack the rest of the squares similarly, following the layout diagram for the size blanket you are making. Tie each stack with a piece of yarn and number them. Randomly designed blankets will benefit from this step as well, as it creates a more even feel to the randomness.
    If your work space allows, you also can design blankets by laying out all of your squares on the floor in the order that you like. Then stack your rows, bundle, and number them.

STEP 2

joining options

Once you have decided on the quantity and colors of the squares you will be using to make a blanket, you next need to decide how to join them. There are two ways to sew the squares together, and this decision should be based on the quality of the felt you have acquired from your processed sweaters.

Method One: *If your material is thick, holds a crisp edge, and is not raveling at all when roughed up, you can butt the edges together using the ladder stitch variation (see page 30).*

Method Two: *If your material is a little stretchier and slightly ravelly on the edges, it is best to overlap the edges and use a running stitch (see page 28). The running stitch is faster and leaves a slightly less finished look.*

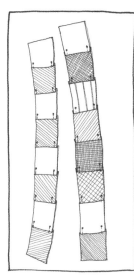

STEP 3

3. Decide how your squares should be joined (see Joining Options, on the previous page). If you need to overlap the squares' edges, do so at both ends by ½". *Note:* The overlap will consume some of the size of each square, and hence the finished blanket. It is perfectly acceptable to add a row and/or column to your finished blanket to have the finished size match the standard shown on the diagram.

SEWING

4. Thread your needle with Persian wool, embroidery floss, or another wool sewing yarn.

5. Sew the squares into strips using the stitch you have decided upon. Be sure you catch both pieces with each stitch, and that you are not sewing so close to the edge that the stitches will pull out. The bigger the blanket, the more wear and tear there will be on the seams based on the physical weight of the finished piece. You can choose to conceal the knots (see page 28) or use them as a decorative accent.

the finishing touch

There are several techniques that can be used to finish your blanket. The simplest is to just leave it as it is and call it done. However, I am a stickler for more durable finished edges, and I relish the opportunity to introduce a pop of unexpected color and texture to my work. Think carefully about what you choose. If the blanket is going to be used on a bed or by a baby, a luscious edge of velvet or silk is an asset to behold. You can buy new yardage at a fabric store, or check your thrift shops for garments made of the fabric you like. Soft and pliable flannel, cotton jersey, velvet, and silk work best. Don't worry too much about the style of

the garments you choose. Just look for the texture you would like against your upper lip and buy accordingly. Buy more cloth than you think you will need. (For approximate edging length required, see page 56.)

6. Connect the lengthwise strips together with the same technique used for connecting the squares, matching up the intersections neatly.

7. Steam iron the finished blanket, being sure to add extra steam at the seams to make a nice flat finish.

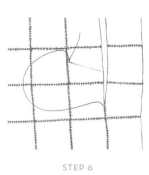

STEP 6

MAKING OPTIONAL EDGING FOR YOUR BLANKET

8. Launder all the material, new or used. Cut the fabric into 3"-wide strips as long as you can make them, including any details from recycled or salvaged garments if you are using them. If you are using woven fabric, cut it on the bias.

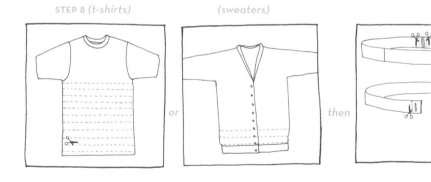

STEP 8 *(t-shirts)*   *(sweaters)*   *or*   *then*

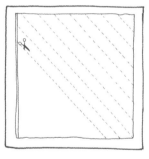

STEP 8 — *for bias (woven fabrics)*

9. With right sides together, running stitch the short ends of the strips together with a small needle and thread to make one long "ribbon" of edging. If you have a variety of edging material, mix up the textures and colors as desired and running stitch a length of the mixed fabrics long enough to bind the perimeter of your blanket.

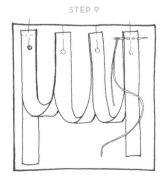

STEP 9

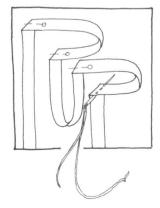

STEP 9 — *for bias*

STEP 11

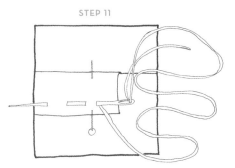

10. If your edging fabric is made from cotton jersey, or other nonravelly cloth, you can skip this step, but most fabrics will need to be ironed. Steam iron the back of the fabric, folding both of the long edges in ¾" toward the middle. (*Note:* If you are using velvet, put a towel down on the ironing board, place the right side of the velvet face down on top of the towel, and press the edges in. You never want to touch the right side of the velvet with the iron.)

Finishing

STEP 12

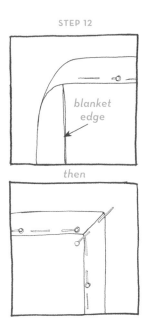

blanket edge

then

11. Once you have enough cloth cut and ironed, fold the strip in half lengthwise with the right side of the fabric out. Starting somewhat in the center between two blanket corners, pin folded strips to the edge of the blanket, being certain that you are inserting the edge of the blanket all the way into the fold of the binding and catching the front and back of the edging material with each pin.

12. When you reach a corner, fold the material as shown to make a mitered corner, pinning both sides of the miter at the corner. When you get back to the beginning, cut off any excess material straight across, allowing for a 2" overlap. Fold the cut edge under about ½" and pin it in place.

13. Thread needle with yarn. Begin sewing at one corner, using a running stitch close to the folded side of the blanket binding (away from the outside edge of the blanket). Check to be sure you are catching the material on both sides of the blanket.

STEP 13

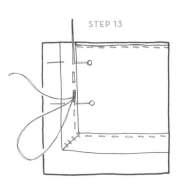

Stitch miters in place as you come across them at each corner.

Blind stitch the folded end in place.

CHAPTER 4

HAND-ME-DOWN
MY NEW
SWEATERS

The first sweater I ever made was a funny collage of different-length sleeves and colorful patterns. The material I used was heavy, wind blocking, and very warm. It was designed as my stargazing sweater — something I could put on over my indoor clothes to pop out onto my patio into the evening air and see the stars — a fitted blanket of sorts.

All the beautiful sweaters I came across in my quest to recycle inspired the development of this collection. After washing and drying, the selected sweaters are usually too small to be worn by adults, yet the fabrics and components are lovely and still very useful. Creating "new from used" allows the maker to bring together different components into a fine collage of

COLOR, TEXTURE, COMFORT, AND FUNCTION.

Sweaters used to make these new collage sweaters should be soft, especially in areas that come in contact with skin, like neck edges and cuffs. They should not be too thick or at all ravelly.

When designing a sweater, consider the wearer and his or her climate. Will it be worn inside or out? Use more densely felted sweaters to make outerwear and thinner, lighter-weight knits for garments to be worn indoors or in temperate climates. Next, consider the shape of the person who will be wearing the sweater. For someone small and tiny, you will choose sweaters that are small and tiny. For a larger and more round person, who probably would not like to have attention brought to the body's fullest areas, go for low-contrast colors, mixed neutrals, or monochromatic sweaters, and be sure the finished sweater is not tight.

To make a sweater in the style and fit you want, read through the section before you decide which style you prefer. You can add hoods, pockets, collars (see chapter 5, page 106), zippers, bell sleeves, thumb holes, gathers, or pleats to your sweater, although beginners might want to start with the basic pullover before getting fancy. Whatever variation you start with, feel free to mix and play with texture, pattern, and yarn and cloth color — even more than might be your nature. The sizing on all of these styles can be easily adapted to make smaller-size sweaters for kids, too.

THE BASIC PULLOVER SWEATER

Making a Basic Pullover is a great beginner project because you're able to stay focused on learning the technique without worrying about getting a perfect fit. Making the Basic Pullover requires only three felted or "foundation" sweaters, however it's better to have six sweaters that you can use bits of for the best, most interesting finished product.

.

you will need

» A favorite pullover-style garment to use for a pattern

» 3 to 6 felted wool sweaters of similar weight

» Sharp fabric scissors or a rotary cutter and pad

» Extra-long straight pins

» A few yarn darner needles in sizes 14–18

» Persian wool (or similar) sewing yarn in 3 or 4 colors

» Ruler or T square

SELECTION AND CUTTING

Selecting the Middle Panel

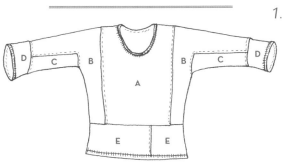

GENERAL LAYOUT

1. Start by choosing the felted sweater best suited for the middle panel A of your new sweater. This panel is the building block of the rest of the sweater. Choose the best piece you have for this, keeping the following things in mind:

    *   The middle panel is the most visible part of the sweater, both front and back.
    *   It should have a nice neckline or one that can be altered to make a nice neckline. Easy alterations are limited to making the existing neck hole bigger. (See No-regrets Necks, page 75.)
    *   To make an adult-size sweater, the middle panel of your felted sweater should be pretty big — at least 15" across, from armpit to armpit.
    *   It is important that the sweater for the middle panel, in particular, is one that holds a firm cut edge well.
    *   It should be a color you (or the recipient) like to wear.
    *   It should NOT have a plunging V-neck or some sort of a weird cowl.

Cutting the Middle Panel

2. Once you have selected the felted sweater for the middle panel A, flatten it out neatly on your work surface, being sure that the side seams are placed evenly at the sides and the sweater is smooth. If there is a waistband that pulls the bottom edge of the sweater in,

selecting your pattern garment

For this simple pullover, I suggest finding a simple-shaped garment to use as your pattern. I like to use my husband's sweatshirts for patterns. We call him Biggie; he is 6' 4" and solid. His sweatshirts fit him just below the waist, not tight throughout but fitting his form. When I try on this garment, it is big on me. The sleeves are too long and the waistband pulls in and is unflattering, but it is easy to use the sweatshirt as a base. To achieve the style I want, I plan for shorter sleeves and to leave off the waistband. When making a sweater for my hubby, I can use the same pattern garment and make different adjustments to accommodate his desired fit. In addition to fit, the pattern garment gives an idea of "drape" or finished garment weight. Again, you can use the pattern garment as a base, changing the weight of the finished garment when selecting the felted sweaters you will use.

keeping the side seam from being straight from armpit to hem, cut the waistband off. To do this, make a small hole with your scissors at the edge where the waistband joins the body of the sweater. Insert your scissors through the little hole and carefully cut the waistband off, cutting one layer at a time and making sure that the cut is accurate.

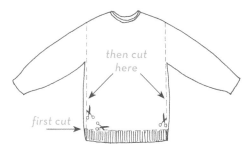

STEPS 2 & 3

3. With the first felted sweater neatly flattened on your work surface and side seams evenly laid out at garment edges, create the middle panel of your new sweater by cutting off the side seams and sleeves with scissors or a rotary cutter. Make the panel as wide as possible (at least 15" for an adult size), and be sure your cut lines are straight, using a ruler or T square to make a 90-degree angle from the bottom edge to the side of the panel. Check to be sure that the distance between the cut edge and the neck hole are even on either side. (I use my hands to measure for this step, but you might want to rely on a ruler or measuring tape.)

Selecting Sleeve Tops and Side Panels B

4. Lay your pattern garment out flat on your work area, paying careful attention to be certain that side seams are lined up smooth and tidy at the sides. With your freshly cut middle panel A folded neatly at shoulder seams, place it in the center of the pattern garment, matching neck holes and measuring to be sure it is centered properly.

    Select a second felted sweater for two sleeve tops and side panels B. These pieces should be:

    * *A similar weight and texture to the middle panel sweater.*
    * *Long enough to match the length of the middle panel sweater from shoulder to bottom cut edge.*

    Hold sweater B on top of pattern garment and panel A to see if the size is right. Keep in mind that if there is a waistband or cuffs cinching in the bottom of the sweater or sleeves, it is best to carefully cut them off in the same way as described above (see step 2).

STEP 4

STEP 5 — side 1

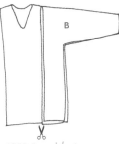

STEP 5 — side 2

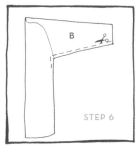

STEP 6

STEP 6 DETAILS:

Cutting Sleeve Top and Side Panels B

5. Smooth sweater piece B in place on one side of the middle panel, matching the side seam and shoulder edge up with the edges of pattern sweater. Allowing for ½" overlap with panel A, carefully cut from bottom edge of sweater B to the shoulder. Use this cut panel B as a pattern for the other side by placing it face down on top of the other side, carefully matching edges and right sides. Cut second panel from sweater B, carefully following the cut edge of the first panel. You will now have a left and right panel cut from sweater B. Place the two panel B pieces on either side of panel A, on top of your pattern garment, matching up outside edges.

   Note: The next two steps are used to make the sleeves wide enough. Occasionally it is not needed because the sleeves of sweater B are as wide as those on the pattern garment. Even if sweater B sleeves are as wide as the pattern garment sleeves, you *can* add the panel C pieces as a design element if desired. If you are not using these pieces, skip ahead to step 8.

Remove Underarm Seams from Panels B

6. On each panel B piece, carefully cut from cuff edge toward armpit right next to the seam. Continue cutting past the armpit down the side seam, stopping 1" from where the panel hits the sleeve edge of the pattern garment.

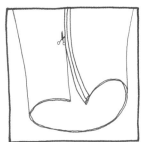

First, cut along one side of seam.

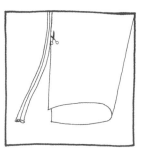

Then cut along other side of seam.

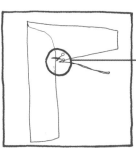

Finish 1" past armpit; clip and remove old seam strip.

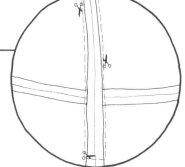

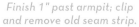

Beginning at the cuff edge a second time, cut along the same distance on the other side of the seam. When you reach the end of the previous cut, snip off the long strip, removing it completely from your work.

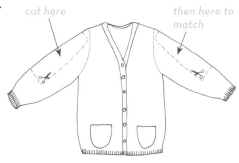

cut here

then here to match

Selecting and Cutting Panels C for Under Sleeves

7. You need a set of matching sleeves for panels C. The fabric should be thin and drape well. I usually use the top of felted-sweater sleeves since they are longer than the underarm length, and there are usually no seams detracting from the drapability of the fabric.

   To determine length for panel C, measure one panel B piece from cuff edge to armpit, and decide how much width you want to add to the finished sleeve. Add 1" seam allowance on all sides.

   With your felted sweater laid out smoothly, cut a long rectangle from the top of one of the sleeves, using your desired finished measurements as a guide but cutting it bigger than you think you need. Use this first panel as a pattern for making a second panel C from the other sleeve.

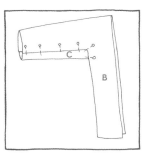

STEP 8

Insert Panels C

8. Neatly fold the panel C pieces in half lengthwise. Place one panel C under each panel B piece on your pattern garment, tucking it neatly inside the underarm opening you made. Adjust the sleeve width as desired. Pin panels B and C together with panel B overlapping panel C by about ½". (Any excess fabric on panel C can be trimmed away later.) Place pins horizontal to the cut edge to keep finger stabbing to a minimum. Be sure you are pinning through only one layer of each panel B and C. Pin front and back. Repeat with the other sleeve.

Preparing Panel D

9. Depending on the size of your pattern sweater and your felted "foundation" sweaters, this piece may not be necessary. It is good to know how to lengthen sleeves in any event. Two panel Ds are made from

STEP 9

the bottoms of matching sweater sleeves that are long and wide enough to match your pattern garment sleeve. Comfort is key for D. Use soft, nonscratchy material, and be sure the cuffs are neither too tight nor too loose around the wrist.

Lay sweater D on top of your pattern garment, adjusting the placement as needed to carefully match the total sleeve width formed by pieces B and C. Add ½" for overlap; panel D will be sewn inside the cut edges of B and C. Cut D straight across once you are sure the pieces will fit accurately. If the sleeve turns out to be too long when you match D to B and C, you can trim off the excess length from the cuff edge, or fold the excess cuff edge to the outside stitch down. Use the first panel D as a pattern to cut the second one.

Preparing Bottom Panel E

10. Bottom panel E is usually made from two or three different sweaters. (These pieces can be made from leftover sweater bits.) Measure the distance from the bottom edge of your pattern garment to the bottom of panels A and B. Cut panel E pieces to match this measurement plus an inch or two. The pieces should all be the same height, but the lengths can vary. Remove any side seams. You will need to join together enough pieces to go around the full circumference of the garment pattern, plus a couple of inches.

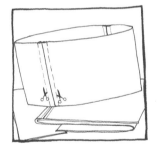

STEP 10 — *removing side seams*

SEWING

Joining Panels B and C

11. Thread a yarn darner needle with wool yarn in the color of your choice and knot the end. Beginning at the sleeve end, stick your needle between pieces B and C and push it up through B. Pull it through. (The yarn is now coming out from the right side of the fabric of panel B.) While carefully holding the edges of B and C together

with ½" overlap, insert the needle in the bottom of panel C wrapping your yarn around the outside edge as you come back up through both layers right below your first stitch. (I call this wrapping layers.) This first step keeps your knot concealed (see page 28).

Join panels B and C completely by sewing with a running stitch all the way up to the armpit, down the side seam to the turning point, and back along the other side to the sleeve end. I often make a decorative double, in-place, or reinforced X stitch at stress points, or where seams need a little extra hold for neatness. When you get to the end, make a double stitch, knot the yarn off on the inside of the garment and hide and trim the end. Repeat on the other sleeve.

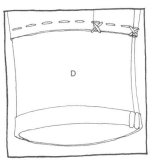

STEP 12

Attaching Panel D

12. Now add panel D to the mix. Carefully tuck the cut edge of panel D inside the sleeve opening created by B and C; they should overlap about ½". Start sewing at the place where B and C meet to strengthen that intersection, conceal your knot, and make a reinforced X stitch. Sew around the sleeve with a running stitch, paying attention not to stitch any puckers in place. To avoid puckers, ease the materials together as described on page 27. Repeat on the other sleeve.

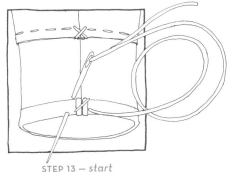

STEP 13 — *start*

Finishing Cuff Edges

13. Depending on length, the cuffs can either be left alone or turned back and ladder stitched in place. Ladder stitching allows for stretch, which is important here. To ladder stitch, fold your cuff edge to the outside ¾". Start the seam by inserting the needle through just the outer layer of the fold. Double stitch, hiding the knot between the folded layers, then begin stitching through both layers, coming straight from point of exit to the next point of entry across the cut edge of the fold.

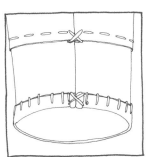

STEP 13 — *finish*

After working all the way around, double stitch, knot your yarn off on the inside, and hide the end.

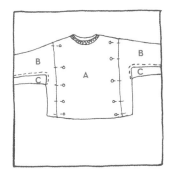

STEP 14

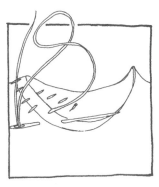

STEP 15

Joining Panel A to Panel B

14. Line up the bottom edges of A with the bottom edges of B. Overlap A on top of B by ½". Pin in place and sew with a running stitch. Conceal your knots at beginning and end. Sew left and right sides in place.

Finishing the Neck Edge

15. Determine the appropriate neck size, fold it down ½", and ladder stitch it in place. Conceal your knots when starting and finishing.

Attaching Panel E Pieces

16. Panel E needs to be constructed and added to finish your sweater. You are making a very long rectangle or strip of cloth that will fit loosely around the hips. Running stitch the short ends of the panels you have cut for E with ½" overlap. Do not conceal your knots here — you will see why in a few minutes.

17. Beginning at one side of your sweater, overlap the A/B panel on top of E by ½", pin in place. Sew with a running stitch, or ladder stitch if your garment is tight-fitting and needs to stretch here. Either way, sew all the way around the sweater, using a reinforced X stitch at the intersection of all panel seams for stability. You may have a little

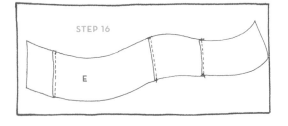

STEP 16

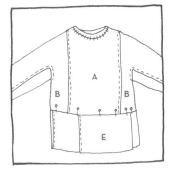

STEP 17 — adding E to A/B

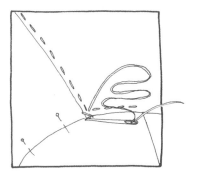

STEP 17 — reinforcing intersections

length left over on E. Tuck the excess neatly inside the beginning edge of E. Join the two pieces by sewing with a running stitch ½" from the outside edge, from midline seam to sweater hem. Do not conceal ending knot.

Finishing the Bottom Edge

18. Fold the bottom edge of your sweater to the outside about ¾" and ladder stitch all the way around the garment. This step conceals all the knots you left showing when working E. When you get back to where you started, conceal your knot.

Finishing Touches

19. Turn sweater inside out and trim off extra length of E and any other excessive overlaps you might have left behind (check C, as that is often bigger than needed). Turn your sweater right side out and try it on!

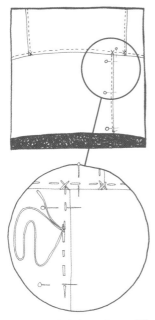

STEP 17 — *joining edges of E*

no-regrets necks

It is much easier to make the neck hole bigger than to try to make it entirely different. If you would like to make the neck hole bigger than it would be if you just simply folded it down and stitched it, there are some things you should know. First and foremost, you

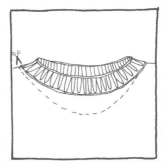

cannot go back and fix it if you make the neck hole too big. Begin by cutting off a small width of the neck edge all the way around. Customarily there is a surged seam that holds neck ribbing in place on most mass-produced

sweaters. If you cut this seam off you, run the risk of having the sweater you are creating turn into a wide-necked Flashdance-esque garment that will likely drive you nuts when it keeps falling off your shoulders. Keep in mind that most men like to wear things that rest comfortably on their shoulders, so if you are making this sweater for a specific person, you might want to ask about neckline preferences before you start. You can cut the entire neck ribbing off if the sweater is firmly felted and the existing neck hole is teeny tiny. Just do keep in mind that sweaters are really stretchy and you should make the neck hole, if you are adjusting it, smaller than you think, as it will grow as you handle it.

ZIPPERED CARDIGAN

This zipper technique seems almost magical to me. Prior to developing this foolproof way to put in a zipper, I always had trouble making them look the way I wanted — tidy and even. You can use this technique to put in a full zipper, as I describe here, or adapt it for half zips or even pocket zippers.

This project starts with a completed Basic Pullover (see pages 66–75). You may or may not have added pockets already (see pages 96–101). Now you will add a zipper, turning a pullover into a cardigan.

you will need

» A completed Basic Pullover (see pages 66–75)
» A separating zipper the length of the garment you are making or slightly longer
» Measuring tape
» Extra-long straight pins
» A size 14 yarn darner needle
» Persian wool sewing yarn, reduced to 2-ply instead of the standard 3-ply

» Sharp fabric scissors
» Small scrap of coordinating felted wool for zipper pull

optional

» Clear acrylic plastic piece about 5" × 18" (see A Tip for Adding Zippers, page 79)

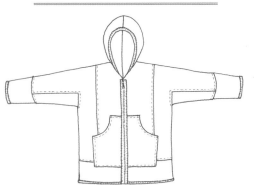

GENERAL LAYOUT

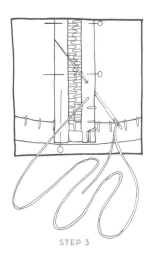

STEP 3

PREPARING YOUR MATERIALS

1. Lay your completed Basic Pullover out flat, neat, and even.

2. With zipper pull at top, lay the zipper out on the sweater front, with the bottom edges flush. (Don't worry if the zipper is an inch or two longer than the sweater at the top.) Measure to be sure it runs right down the middle of the sweater. It is fine if it crosses the center of a kangaroo-pouch pocket. If you have added patch or welt pockets, the zipper should be centered between them. (For pocket instructions, see pages 96–101.) Beginning from the bottom, pin the zipper in place with the bottom edge of the zipper flush with the bottom edge of the sweater. Place pins every two inches to ensure the zipper is flat against the sweater front. Any excess zipper length should be at the top.

SEWING ZIPPER IN PLACE

3. Thread the needle with yarn. Conceal your knot by sewing up through the bottom tab of the zipper only, about ½" in from both the bottom of the sweater and zipper and the side of the zipper. Wrap the bottom edge of the zipper and sweater with one or two strong stitches coming out of the same hole in the zipper tab each time. Then wrap the side edge of the zipper by taking a stitch into just the sweater, right next to the zipper, and again coming out of the same hole in the zipper tab.

4. Once you have the zipper securely fastened, ladder stitch along one edge of the zipper; leave the pins in as you go. Be sure to go through all the layers of fabric that constitute the front of the sweater, especially if you are traversing a pocket. But be careful not to sew right through the back of the sweater too!

5. If there is excess zipper length at the top, stop sewing 2" from the top of the sweater. Position the zipper pull down a few inches, then cut the excess zipper to just 1" to 2" above the top of the sweater. Use caution when snipping off the top of the zipper because if the pull comes off, it is not easy to get it back on the track. Fold the excess under and continue to ladder stitch to the top, being sure to catch both layers of the zipper edge in each stitch. Double stitch at the top and conceal the knot.

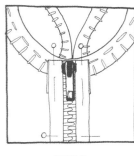

STEP 5

Sew up the other side of the zipper in place, in the same manner as the first side, beginning at the bottom.

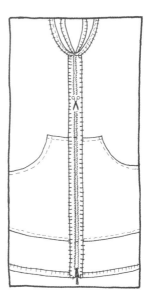

STEP 6

FINISHING

6. Once you have both sides sewn in place, remove the pins and completely unzip the zipper. Using your fabric scissors, carefully cut from the bottom edge of the sweater right up the middle between the two sides of the zipper. (This is sort of like bowling with bumpers; it is really easy to cut and pretty impossible to make a mistake.) Voila! You have a super cool zipper in place!

7. Cut a narrow strip of coordinating wool about 1" × 6". Thread one end through the zipper pull and knot it, creating a decorative zipper pull.

✳ *a tip for adding zippers*

I have a 5" × 18" piece of clear acrylic that the child of an employee made for me 15 years ago. When stitching zippers in place, I put the clear acrylic inside the sweater and sew against it. It keeps me from accidentally going through the back of the sweater and makes it easier to sew the zippers (or hook and eye tape, see pages 84–86) in truly flat. I find it helpful when adding pockets or embellishing with embroidery too. I highly recommend one! (If you want to see how it works, try using a CD jewel case; the bigger size works better, though.)

EMPIRE VEST
WITH GATHERS

The Empire Vest is cute and easy to construct. It is designed to fit snuggly on top with a gracefully skirted bottom.

The most flattering way to make sweaters that gather is quite simple: The lower, gathered part of the garment you are making must be lightweight and flowing. So be sure to pick fine-gauge sweater material that lends itself best to movement and easy draping.

you will need

» At least 4 felted wool sweaters — one tightly felted that will fit your bodice, one with wide, sturdy ribbing, and the others thin with nice drape for the skirted bottom
» Sharp fabric scissors or a rotary cutter and pad
» Permanent felt-tip marker
» Ruler
» Extra-long straight pins

» A few yarn darner needles in sizes 14–18
» Persian wool (or similar) sewing yarn in 3 or 4 colors
» ½ yard hook and eye tape

optional

» Clear acrylic insert (see A Tip for Adding Zippers, page 79)

GENERAL LAYOUT

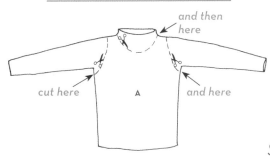

and then here

cut here

and here

STEP 1

STEP 2

SELECTION AND CUTTING

Selecting and Cutting Panel A

1. Find a well-felted sweater that fits the way you would like the top of your empire vest to fit, preferably a little snug. Without concern for precision, cut off the sleeves and neck edges so you can try it on and be sure you like the fit.

2. Once you have decided on the right sweater for panel A, even out the neck and armhole edges, leaving seam allowances of ½" to fold over and stitch down later.

   Measure from the top of your shoulder to where you would like to have the top panel stop on your body (or the body that you are making the sweater to fit). Measure front and back and mark, with either a felt-tip marker or straight pins, the length plus ½" for a seam allowance. Cut the bottom off carefully, using the marker lines (or pins) as a measurement and cutting through just one layer at a time.

Selecting and Cutting Panel B

3. Panel B is made from the ribbing at the bottom of a second felted sweater. I like to use the widest and most felted band I can find. If one length of ribbing is not enough, you can join the short ends of two of similar weight and texture with a running stitch. You could even make this band from a handful of opened cuffs (with seams removed), using a running stitch to join them.

STEP 3

Selecting and Cutting Panel C

The panel C pieces become the skirt and are most successful if made from very thin, lightweight sweaters. The number of panels needed is determined by the width you are able to cut them, and the desired finished size. Measure the length you would like to make the garment by trying on what you have chosen for panels A and B and measuring from the bottom of panel B to where you would like the hem to fall.

4. Neatly flatten your selected sweaters on your workspace table, being sure that the side seams are evenly placed at the sides and the bottom edges are tidy and even. Trim off any ribbing that pulls the sweater in at the bottom.

5. Measure from the bottom of the sweaters you have chosen for C toward the neck edge and, with a felt-tip marker or pin, mark desired length plus ½". If this mark falls short of the armpits of the sweaters used for C, cut straight across through both layers. (If the sweater was a cardigan, you will have a very long and large rectangle. If the sweater was a pullover, cut the tube open along one of the side seams, removing the seam completely.) If, however, the mark falls closer to the neck edges of the sweaters being used for C than the armpits, cut from the sweater hem edge along both side seams and then straight across, yielding two large rectangles of fabric. (If you have used a marker, be sure to cut just inside your marked line, carefully removing the black marker lines.)

   Sweaters often taper in from the hem to armpit. This tapering adds to the fullness of the skirt of the Empire Vest. If you would like to increase the flare, trim the large rectangles to taper on one end.

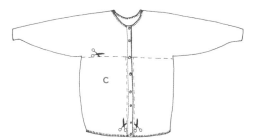

STEP 5 — *cutting at armpits*

STEP 5 — *cutting above armpits*

CRISPINA'S
DESIGN NOTES

Sleeves can also be used for panel C of the Empire Vest. While it is often difficult to find sleeves long enough, when you do, they can be opened along the seam, which should be removed completely (see page 70).

STEP 6

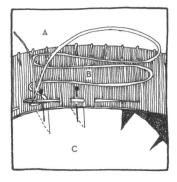

STEP 7

STEP 8

SEWING

Stitching Panel A to Panel B

6. Pin panels A and B together, with B overlapping A by ½". Be sure to spread out any length in panel A to ease the seam smooth.

   Thread a needle with Persian wool yarn. Begin sewing at a side seam of panel A, with panel B on top, then conceal your knot (see page 28) and carefully ladder stitch the panels together all the way around.

Attaching Panel C

7. With a single ply of Persian wool, attach the pieces you have for panel C using a running stitch, making sure you have all the narrower ends on the same side; this will produce a flared skirt panel.

   Along the shorter (top) edge of panel C, snip cuts 1" deep every 3".

8. Mark the center front of panel B with a pin. Pin one end of panel C at this center point to panel B. Work your way around, overlapping the fabric ½" and pinning in place at each snip. At center back, change the direction of the overlap to be sure the pleats are symmetrical on either side of the center line. This will make the skirted bottom open. If you prefer a closed skirt, attach C to B at a side seam rather than center front, which will make your finish overlap less conspicuous. In that case, allow for ½" overlap and running stitch it closed (see Empire Vest Variation, page 86).

   Once you have the skirt pinned in place, running stitch it to B, being careful to secure each gather in two places.

Attaching the Hook and Eye Tape

9. Cut a piece of hook and eye tape to match the length of the front, beginning ½" below the cut neck edge and extending to the bottom of panel B. (*Note:* Before you cut the tape, be sure that you have an

equal — and generous — length of tape without a hook or eye on it at both the top and bottom.)

Center the tape on the front of panel A. (Check with your ruler to be sure it is centered at both the top and bottom.) Fold under the tape's fabric ends at the bottom of panel B and pin folded edge flush with the bottom of B through both layers of the folded tape and just the top layer of fabric. Use several pins to secure the full length of the placket in place.

Thread a size-14 yarn darner with 2 yards of wool sewing yarn, and knot one end with an overhand knot. Begin sewing by inserting the needle from the back of panel B on one side, coming through the front about ½" from the bottom and the side of the tape placket. Double stitch around the bottom and side edges of the right side of the tape placket. Put the clear acrylic insert between the layers of panel A/B, if desired. Ladder stitch up the right side of the closure tape, sewing against the piece of clear acrylic as you go, allowing the work to lay flat on the work surface. Finish off the seam with a concealed ending knot. Repeat for other side.

CRISPINA'S
DESIGN NOTES

I used a super heavy-duty hook and eye tape as a closure on this piece; it is available in a variety of styles and materials including cotton poly, satin, and velvet, and it adds nicely to the look. The tape features a continuous length of hooks (on one side) and eyes (on the other) attached to reinforced tape or fabric; it is added in the same way as a zipper (see Zippered Cardigan, pages 76–79). You can find it, or something similar, at lots of places online. It is normally sold by the yard.

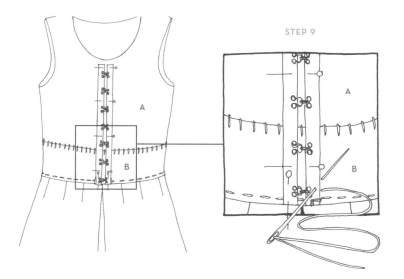

STEP 9

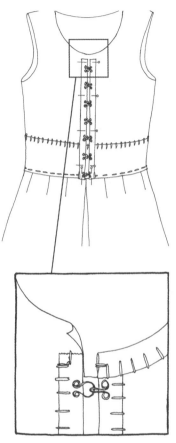

STEP 10

Finishing Touches

10. Fold the neck edge of the sweater to the outside about ½". Beginning at the center of the neck edge, make the first double stitch through one side of closure tape placket. Using a ladder stitch, work around the neck edge and end by securing the other side of the closure tape placket.

11. Fold the armhole edges to the outside about ½". Ladder stitch the armholes, beginning at bodice side seam.

12. Open all the hooks and eyes. Cut the sweater along the path between the left and right sides of the closure tape, beginning at the bottom and continuing right up and through the neck edge.

Just like magic, your Empire Vest is now open in the front and finished!

EMPIRE VEST VARIATION

» *Make a pullover vest.* By skipping the front hook and eye option closure altogether, you can make a pullover vest, as shown on the facing page. This variation translates nicely to child-size dresses (as shown) and can even be worked into a dress/vest for an adult, too. It looks nice to center one panel C piece in the front of the garment, filling the rest of the skirt circumference with two, or sometimes three, other panels.

Add a collar, even out of
a patchwork of pieces!

Pockets can
customize the
look, too!

Skip the closure and
make the vest a pullover
or a dress.

Add ribbing pieces
at hem for an under-
skirt look.

RENAISSANCE TOP WITH BELL SLEEVES

I made the first Renaissance Top when I was quite pregnant and off to a local retail show. I made the skirted bottom extra roomy. It was comfy, concealed the bursting waistband beneath, and looked dressy and flattering. I should have had a dozen others to sell at that show, but since then I have made lots. They are not designed to be maternity wear but do work well for that purpose. The Renaissance Top is obviously designed for women.

The bell sleeves are created by combining sleeves from two different sweaters, with the lower piece placed upside down. You will not need a pattern garment for this sweater.

you will need

- » 4 to 5 felted wool sweaters — one tightly felted that will fit your bodice, one with wide, sturdy ribbing, and the others thin with nice drape for the skirted bottom and bell sleeves (*Note:* The flared skirt of this sweater is normally created from five or six felted garment sleeves — in pairs or all different.)
- » Permanent felt-tip marker
- » Ruler
- » Sharp fabric scissors or a rotary cutter and pad
- » Extra-long straight pins
- » A few yarn darner needles in sizes 14–18
- » Persian wool (or similar) sewing yarn in 3 or 4 colors

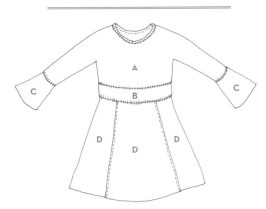

GENERAL LAYOUT

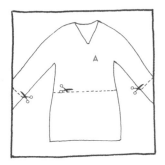

STEP 1

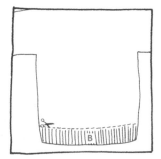

STEP 2

SELECTION AND CUTTING

Selecting and Cutting Panel A

1. Choose a felted sweater that fits comfortably through the top and arms. This will be used for panel A.

   Put it on and measure from the top of your shoulder to where you would like to have the top panel stop on your body (or the body that you are making the sweater to fit). Measure front and back, marking the length you desire plus ½" with a felt-tip marker or pins. Measure and mark 2" below your elbows.

   Remove the sweater and, following the marks or pins, cut off the bottom of the sweater and the bottom of the sleeves, being careful to cut off the marker lines as you go.

Selecting and Cutting Panel B

2. Panel B is made from the bottom ribbing of a sweater. I like to use the widest and most densely felted band I can find. Choose one that will fit snug but comfortably. If one length of ribbing is not long enough, you can join the short ends of two with a running stitch.

Joining Panels A and B

3. Pin panel B over A with a ½" overlap all the way around. You may need to ease (see page 27) the pieces together a bit if A is longer than B. Be careful to spread the easing evenly around the circumference of the garment; any puckering can be steamed out later.

Selecting and Cutting Panel C

4. The panels for C are made from a pair of matching sleeves wide enough at the cuff end to match the width of panel A's sleeves and flared enough to drape the way you like. In most cases, any cuff ribbing will need to be removed to make C fit inside the sleeve of A smoothly. Find the point at which the lower sleeve of sweater C

matches the width of sleeve A; measure from that point toward the armpit of sweater C, add 1" to the length, and cut panel C. (I like bell sleeves to nearly cover my hands when they rest down at my sides. It is easy to make the sleeves shorter later if you want.) Match up the sleeve seams and tuck the narrower end of C neatly up inside the cut sleeve end of A with ½" overlap. Pin in place, and repeat with the other sleeve.

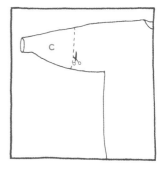

STEP 4

Selecting and Cutting Panel D

5. The flared bottom of the Renaissance Top can range in length and fullness significantly, so determine how long you would like yours to be. Make an estimate by measuring where B ends on your body to where you would like the bottom of the sweater to fall. (If you are a daredevil, you can carefully try on your work-in-progress project — full of pins — and get an actual measurement.) I usually make a rough estimate of length because I normally use four or five sleeves for this panel, and so the length is "predetermined" by the shortest sleeve. (Feel free to use the sleeves in pairs, or not.)

STEP 5

6. Open each panel D sleeve by cutting along the seam, and then remove the seam completely as described on page 70. Keep the cuffs intact until you see what you have. If the cuffs are removed completely, you won't need as many panels and the skirt will be more tapered. Keeping the cuffs on creates a fuller, more swingy look, and the possibility of a longer skirt.

Stack all the sleeves together, identify the shortest one (which determines the skirt length), and trim all the other panels to match. Select one piece to feature as center panel D. Select a second panel and, with cuff edges together, pin it to the center panel, with the center panel edge on top. Running stitch them together with a standard ½" overlap. Add a third panel on the other side of the center panel and join with a running stitch. Once you have these three panels

CRISPINA'S
DESIGN NOTES

There are two options for finishing the neckline. For neckline shown above, panel A can be cut and folded down like the Empire Vest description on page 82. To add a collar as shown in the other Renaissance Tops, follow the directions for collars on pages 106–108.

sewn together, pin the center panel D to panel B (matching centers exactly). Determine how many additional panels you need (if any) to complete the skirt. When you have the circumference of panel D complete, leave the last seam open. Attach D to B with a ladder stitch, with B overlapping D. When you get all the way around B, sew down the last Panel D seam with a running stitch.

SEWING

Joining Panels A and B

7. With wool sewing yarn, stitch A and B together with a ladder stitch.

Attaching Panel C

8. Ladder stitch the sleeve edge of A onto the tucked in edge C. Begin at the matched up seams and continue around. Conceal your start and finish knots.

Attaching Panel D

9. Running stitch panel D pieces together to create a large flared panel, leaving the last seam open. Carefully center the panel you have chosen to be in front, and pin B over D all the way around, overlapping by ½". Also leave a ½" overlap at the end so the skirt can be closed at completion. Ladder stitch B to D. Running stitch D closed from ribbing band to hem.

Finishing Touches

10. Leave cut edges at bottom of sleeves and flared skirt raw and unfinished, allowing the fabric to move and flow more easily than it would if those edges were finished in any other way. Steam iron seams flat.

CHAPTER 5

MIX-AND-MATCH SWEATER ADD-ONS

Once the basic technique of sweater construction is established, there are

MANY WAYS
TO CUSTOMIZE YOUR SWEATERS

by adding elements that make the finished product either more useful, fashion-forward, or both. In this chapter pockets, hoods, and collars are the focus. Each of these Add-Ons is an option for any finished sweater, alone or in combination. Feel free to use and vary these techniques in any way you feel inspired.

The pocket designs can be varied greatly in both size and choice of cloth. If you plan to use pockets as hand warmers, the material should be cozy and the placement comfortable to use. Plan the size of your pockets to accommodate whatever contents are planned. Cute little pockets can add a decorative element of fun and be made of nearly any sort of cloth. Larger pockets intended to be used to carry heavy things like keys or change require slightly heavier, more densely felted fabric and should be used on garments of the same texture and density. Most pockets can be cut from scrap material.

Hoods are another fun element to give a whole different feel and look to a sweater. In addition to color, the most important design element in a hood is fit and function. You will learn to make hood patterns to fit any size head.

Cashmere is a wonderful soft cloth to use for hoods, typically offering a thin soft finish. Regular wool hoods have more body and hold shape well, but are not as soft as cashmere. Angora, mohair, and alpaca are very soft but are often 'tickly' next to the skin. Make your fabric selection carefully to add a practical and interesting design element. Most hoods require one whole raw-material sweater to ensure enough fabric.

A collar adds an element of finish and warmth to a wider-necked sweater. As with hoods, collars are often close to the skin, so select soft, nonitchy fabric. Collars made of thin cloth will lie flatter than ones made of thicker material. Ribbing from sweater waste bands make nice collars. It is often necessary to cut the collar wider than the ribbing. If you do this, sew the cut edge inside and let the finished edge of the ribbing become the visible collar edge.

Add a collar.

Pick a pocket style.

Add a hood.

TIME REQUIRED **1 TO 1½ HOURS**
for kangaroo-pouch and patch pockets;
2 TO 2½ HOURS *for welted pockets*

PICK A POCKET

I have used many different kinds of pockets in my sweater making; three basic pocket styles are described here: patch (lower left); kangaroo pouch (top left and lower right); and welt (top right). The pocket style you choose should work with the sweater you have made. The sweaters with skirted bottoms are a little trickier to add pockets to. I suggest starting with simple pullovers that are a great match for all sorts of sweater edits, and they handle pockets with the greatest of ease.

Very light-colored fabric does not lend itself well to pockets. It is often easy to see other colors through it, and it typically looks dirtier faster than darker colored material.

Clockwise from top left: Kangaroo Pocket; Welt Pockets; Kangaroo Pocket; Patch Pockets

you will need

» Flattened cereal box
» A firm, well-felted wool sweater (or 2) with little to no stretch
» Household scissors
» Permanent felt-tip marker
» Sharp fabric scissors

» A yarn darner needle in any size 14–18
» Persian wool (or similar) sewing yarn
» Paper and a pencil to make the pattern
» Steam iron
» Extra-long straight pins
» Ruler

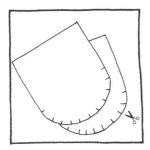

STEP 2

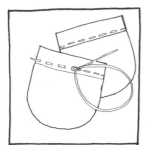

STEP 3

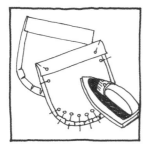

STEP 4

STEP 5

PATCH POCKETS

These are the simplest pocket style I make. They normally come in pairs and can have rounded edges (see photo on page 87), or be simple squares or rectangles. This is a use for extra-heavy felted cloth — no need to fold the edges under. Softer cloth is also useful and will hold up better if you first turn the edges under all the way around, as instructed here. If you're using squares or rectangles, you can skip the whole pattern-making bit and just cut a pair the same shape with rotary cutter and pad.

1. Decide what size you want your pockets. Make a paper pattern the size and shape of the pocket you want to make. (If the shape is symmetrical, you can cut it from a folded piece of paper.) Place the paper pattern on the chosen sweater where you think the pockets will go and see if you like the shape and size. Make necessary adjustments and transfer the pattern to cereal-box cardboard.

2. Trace around the cardboard pattern with the felt-tip marker onto the felted fabric of choice. If the fabric is sturdy with a firm felted texture, it can be cut without seam allowances; most material is not that heavy and requires an extra 1" to turn under at the top and ½" to turn under on the other edges. Cut the pocket out carefully, removing the marker line as you cut. Make small ¼"–⅜" snips in the outer curved edges of the pockets; this will make it easier to turn under and press the edges.

3. Pin under 1" at the top edge and ½" along the curved edges. Press with a steam iron, easing the fabric on curves.

4. Running stitch the top pocket edge.

5. Pin the pocket(s) in place and running stitch the perimeter, excluding the opening. Double stitch the start and end of the seam.

6. Lightly steam the attached pocket.

KANGAROO-POUCH POCKET

Whether or not the sweater you are making has a zipper, the kangaroo-pouch pocket is functional, stylish, and pretty straight-forward. You can make a little kangaroo pouch or a large one depending on the sweater and your aesthetic. If you are planning a cardigan, it is fine to add a pocket now as described here. (You can learn how to make the Zippered Cardigan on pages 76–79.)

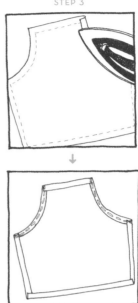

1. Decide what size pocket you want to add to your sweater. Draw the desired shape on a piece of paper, and add ½" all around; this extra will be turned under. Using your household scissors, cut this shape out and place it on the finished pullover sweater where you would like it; check to be sure it is the right shape and size for your garment.

   Trace around the paper onto a flattened cereal box and, using household scissors, cut it out. Now you have your pattern.

2. Trace the pattern onto the fabric of your choice with a felt-tip marker. Cut it out, carefully trimming off the marker line as you go.

3. Fold all the edges under ½", press, and running stitch the hand-entry edges in place. (If you're using heavily felted cloth, you can skip this stitch.)

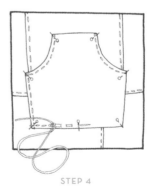

4. Thread the needle with a full strand of Persian yarn. Center the pocket on the sweater front and pin in place. Be sure the pocket falls in a flattering spot, not too high up or low down on the sweater. Running stitch pocket in place. Double stitch pocket corners as well as seam start and finishes for added strength.

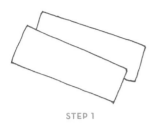

STEP 1

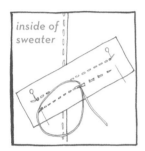

STEP 3

STEP 4

WELT POCKETS

These are the tidiest style pockets, garnering the smoothest and dressiest finish. They are a little complicated but give a lovely result. You can add these to pullovers and cardigans alike. To me, it is important that they come in pairs.

1. Cut two 2" × 6" strips, or plackets, of sturdy but not too thick wool. T-shirt material also works well.

2. Pin these strips, wrong side up, to the wrong side of the garment where you would like pocket openings to be. Pay attention to making the plackets symmetrical and well placed.

3. Make tiny running stitches in two 4" lines, ½" apart, in the center of the plackets. There should be at least ¾" of material on either side of the seams and 1" between the stitches and at the end of the strip on both ends.

4. Cut through both layers of fabric between the lines, being careful not to cut the sewing yarn you used to stitch the placket in place. Cut all the way to the end of the stitch lines but no further.

5. Push the placket fabric through the hole you just cut, turning it right side out on the outside of the sweater.

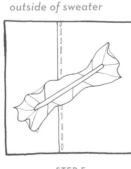

STEP 5

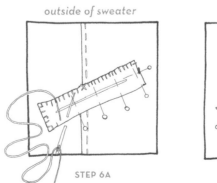

STEP 6A

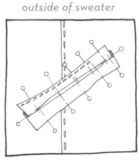

STEP 6B

6. The placket can be finished in one of two ways:

   A. Turn under cut edges and pin neatly, making sure edges are straight and corners square. Using a small and tightly packed ladder stitch, sew edges down all the way around the placket. Reinforce the seam intersection with an X stitch.

   B. Alternately, leave cut edges out and pin in place, making straight edges and square corners. Running stitch in place all the way around the placket.

7. Cut 2 squares or rectangles large enough to cover the opening at top and accommodate your hands below. (These can be cut of pretty much any fabric, and will be visible through the pocket opening.) While considering strength, know also that softer and more snuggly pockets can *make* a garment. Pin in place.

8. Pin squares in place over welt opening on inside of sweater. With a small running stitch, attach the rectangles you just cut to the inside of the garment. The stitching on these will be visible and can add a design element to the finished garment.

POCKET VARIATIONS

» *Big pockets* that hold a lot should be made from sturdy, well-felted material and should be sewn to the same. This type of cloth is not prone to losing its shape and will wear well.

» *Woven fabrics* (see page 18) also make great pockets.

» *Smaller pockets* that are either a design element or used solely for hand warming or holding little things can be made from pretty much any sort of fabric.

outside of sweater

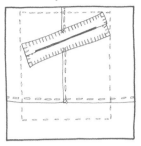

STEP 7

inside of sweater

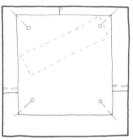

STEP 8

FINISHED POCKETS

HOODS

Hoods are shaped in one basic way. They are designed to cover your head and keep you warm. I find that many commercially made hoods are not really big enough to do their job. (I know, I know, I have a large head and dreadlocks, which take up a lot of room!) Although the instructions describe adding a hood to the Basic Pullover, once you've mastered the technique you can try it on other garments. With this pattern you can make a hood that will fit anyone's head, and add it to almost any sweater you choose.

you will need

» A large paper bag such as a grocery bag for making a pattern (cereal boxes aren't big enough for this pattern)
» Measuring tape
» A completed Basic Pullover (see pages 66–75)
» Household scissors
» Permanent felt-tip marker

» Sharp fabric scissors
» One felted sweater that is soft and on the thin side (there is no better place to use cashmere!)
» A size 14 yarn darner needle
» Extra-long straight pins
» Persian wool (or similar) sewing yarn

SELECTION AND CUTTING

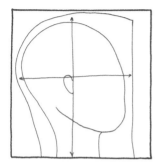

STEP 2

1. Flatten the paper bag and draw a preliminary pattern in the general shape of a hood.

2. Hold the measuring tape on the very top of your head and measure down to where your neck and shoulders meet. Add 1". Measure your pattern drawing and adjust the distance from head to neck edge to match the measurement you took.

   Now measure from the middle of the back of your head to where you would like the front edge to fall. Add 1". Adjust the pattern drawing to accommodate this measurement as well.

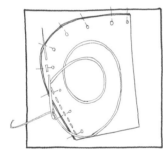

STEP 5

3. Measure the circumference of the neck edge of the finished sweater you will attach the hood to. Divide this number in half and add 1". Adjust the neck edge of hood on the pattern drawing to accommodate this measurement. Cut out the adjusted pattern.

4. Using a felt-tip marker and the pattern you've just created, mark and then cut two mirror-image pieces from the same felted sweater, carefully cutting the marker line off the fabric as you go. (When placing the pattern, it is okay to use ribbing on the neck edge of the hood.)

SEWING

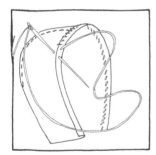

STEP 6

5. Thread the needle with wool sewing yarn. With wrong sides together, running stitch the curved edge of the hood pieces together. Do not conceal knots.

6. Fold back the front edge about ½" and ladder stitch in place. Use reinforced X stitch at the top seam.

7. Pin the hood to the sweater around the neck edge. Begin by tucking the hood inside the neck edge, pinning both front corners carefully in place, centered on the front neck edge. Next pin the joining seam at the back of the hood to the center back of the neck edge. Finally, pin the hood to the inside of the neck edge at halfway points between the center back and the front corner pins on either side. You might find a discrepancy in fabric length between the neck edge and hood edge as you begin to pin them in place. Ease this area by carefully spreading the excess length evenly around the neck edge. If this is a real problem, see Attaching the Hood, Take 2 below.

8. Start sewing with a running stitch at one front corner of the hood and work your way around. If you plan to add a zipper, be sure not to cross your yarn over the front from one hood corner to the other, or it could be cut. If you are adding a hood to a pullover sweater that is tight going over the head, use a ladder stitch to add the hood, which will allow for some stretch.

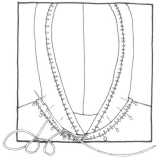

STEP 8

attaching the hood, take 2

The hood can usually be attached to the sweater with a little easing at the seams. Sometimes that's just not enough. Here are several other solutions:

* Leave a gap of up to 3" between the front hood corners.
* Overlap the front hood corners if you are making a pullover style sweater.
* Remove the hood from the sweater, make the necessary adjustments to a newly cut hood, and continue.
* Make necessary adjustments to the hood you have in the works and re-pin it.

COLLARS

Collars can be added to any style sweater. They add a lot of warmth if they cover the neck and shoulders. Collars also make garments seem more finished and present an opportunity to add detail.

you will need

» Sharp fabric scissors
» Sturdy and soft ribbing cut about 4" wide from one extra soft felted sweater
» One completed Basic Pullover (see pages 66–75), Empire Vest with Gathers (see pages 80–87), or Renaissance Top with Bell Sleeves (see pages 88–92)
» Measuring tape
» Extra-long straight pins
» A yarn darner needle in any size 14–18
» Persian wool (or similar) sewing yarn

on collars and seams

There are usually two seams in a loop of ribbing cut from a pullover. If you cut your ribbing from a cardigan, you will likely have two seams and an opening, making a long strip rather than a loop. Either type of ribbing will work for a collar. The key is to center the raw-material seams evenly on your collar panel when cutting it out.

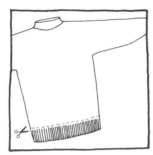

STEP 1

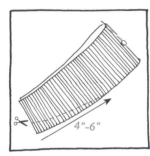

STEP 3

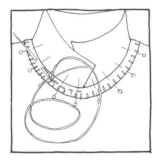

STEP 5

PREPARATION AND CUTTING

1. Cut ribbing from sweater as wide as possible, preferably at least 4". If ribbing is not wide enough, you can cut it slightly wider by including some of the smooth cloth above the ribbing on the raw-material sweater.

2. Measure the circumference of the neck opening of the sweater to which you will be adding a collar. With seams centered, cut your ribbing to the correct length.

3. Hold the front corners of your cut collar panel together and trim off ½" of the cut edge, sloping up to meet the height of the rest of the collar. The slope should be gradual — 4" to 6" between the shorter front edge and the place where it meets the full width of the collar.

4. Pin the front corners of the collar carefully in place inside the neck edge of the sweater; be sure they are centered and even. Pin the center back of the collar panel to the center back of the sweater. Add a few more pins around the neck edge to be sure the collar will be sewn in place evenly without puckers or extra tight spots, easing if necessary.

SEWING

5. Carefully running stitch the collar in place beginning with a double stitch at one front corner and working your way around to the other side. However, if the neck edge is snug going over the head, it would be wise to ladder stitch your collar in place. This will allow for more stretch than a running stitch when being pulled on and off.

CHAPTER 6

CREATING
YOUR OWN
RAGAMUFFIN

The first product I made from recycled wool sweaters was a
RAGAMUFFIN

in 1987. Of course I didn't realize it at the time, but that began my legacy of making and recycling that continues to fill my thoughts many years and creations later.

There are three "old favorite" types of Ragamuffins described here. Dinosaurs were the first species to come into being, the culmination of an art project in college; Potbellies followed to appease customers who wanted a style that could sit down; and the more doll-like Stand-ups are based on the construction technique used for traditional corn husk dolls. Because my production- and design-oriented mind chooses material efficiency over pretty much anything else most of the time, each of the three styles share body components — all Ragamuffins have the same head and tail, and Dinosaurs and Potbellies also have the same kinds of legs.

This chapter is a general lesson in making Ragamuffins. If you follow the directions, you will have a finished creature like the ones that I have been producing and selling for more than 20 years. If you have as much fun as I do with the process and want to get more creative, go ahead! There are many variations on the components and construction process you can develop as you dig in.

Just for starters, once you've mastered the basics, try experimenting with any of the following ideas.

» *Change the scale.* Make people-size creatures with detailed faces, hands, and feet sculpted from all sorts of fabrics and leather or tiny little faeries with no features at all.

» *Incorporate other found materials.* Think about working with other fabrics, buttons, twigs, leaves, moss, bones, plastic bags, and so on.

» *Add wings or an additional pair of legs.*

» *Make clothes for them.*

» *Use the Ragamuffins as puppets* to tell stories of environmentalism and recycling.

Before you know it, you may have invented a whole new creature with its own distinctive name and character!

RAGAMUFFIN BASICS

No matter which style of Ragamuffin you decide to try first, several pieces are common to each figure. Instructions for making those parts — the tail, head, and legs — are given in this section.

Before beginning this process, you will need to collect the felted sweaters you'll be using, prepared according to the guidelines on pages 20–21. Remember, Ragamuffins can be made in any mix of textures, colors, and patterns you like, and some pieces can be cut from leftovers and scraps.

you will need

» 3–6 felted wool sweaters in assorted colors, patterns, textures, and weights
» Sharp fabric scissors or a rotary cutter and pad
» A 10" dinner plate or other 10" circular shape to use as a head pattern
» A size 18 yarn darner needle
» Persian wool or similar sewing yarn in 3 or 4 colors
» Extra-long straight pins
» A handful of buttons to choose from (these can come from the sweaters you have chosen)

» Stuffing material (this can be tiny bits of scrap from the project, wool fleece, or, in a pinch, polyester fiberfill)

optional

» Empty flattened cereal boxes for making pattern pieces
» Permanent felt-tip marker
» Household scissors
» Small spring-loaded pliers

RAGAMUFFIN TAIL

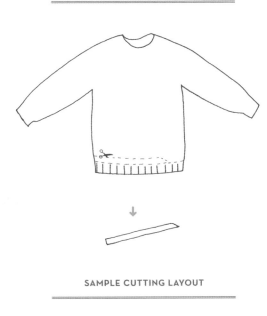

SAMPLE CUTTING LAYOUT

We'll begin with the ending, since all Ragamuffins have the same basic kind of tail. But the look can vary greatly. This is a good place to invoke your creativity. Tails can be cut from other materials, not just textiles — for example, inner tubes from your local bike shop or scrap leather as well as sweater plackets — or tied into big fat knots for bunny-like tails. Thin material from finer knits works best for the traditional-style tail, and you should avoid incorporating any sweater seams. There are just two basic steps.

1. Cut a long, narrow rectangle approximately 1½" × 8" from suitable felted materials.

2. Shape one end to a point with fabric scissors and knot it.

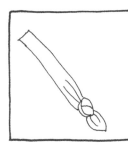

STEP 2   STEP 2 — *knot detail*

work table setup

When cutting Ragamuffins parts, I stand at my worktable, where I also have enough space to sort the pieces into stacks as I cut them. I have a rotary pad on the table and use a rotary cutter for any straight cutting. Curves and double thickness cuts are done with scissors. I have a pincushion handy with needles and pins. I like to cut most of the pieces freehand; if you are concerned about that, or prefer accurate cutting, feel free to make patterns for your components. While this adds another step before beginning, it is fine! I suggest using empty flattened cereal boxes to make cardboard patterns. (See Step: Layout and Cutting, page 22, and Using Patterns, page 39.)

SHORT LEGS FOR DINOSAURS & POTBELLIES

There are just a few things to think about when selecting felted wool for the legs, short or long. Although it can be pretty much any texture, it should not be too open or loosely knit, or apt to unravel. Extra densely felted fabrics and double-knit ski-style sweaters are not great for legs because they are too hard to sew through. But since the felt will be rolled and secured, it's all right to use pieces with small moth holes or other imperfections for the legs.

CUTTING SHORT LEGS

1. For each short leg, cut a small rectangle of felt from any part of an appropriate sweater measuring anywhere between 5" and 8" in width and between 9" and 12" in length. These measurements will make the leg somewhere between 5" and 9" long. (You can also cut a tube from a sleeve about 5" long.)

2. Each pair of legs should be the same length, so cut another rectangle matching the measurements of the first leg piece exactly. However, it's fine to use pairs of different lengths for the Ragamuffins.

CONSTRUCTING THE SHORT LEGS

3. Thread your needle with a piece of sewing yarn about 1½ yards long. Tie a knot in one end.

SAMPLE CUTTING LAYOUT

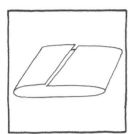

STEP 4

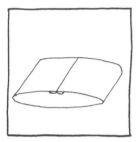

STEP 4 — *sleeve tube*

STEP 5

STEP 6

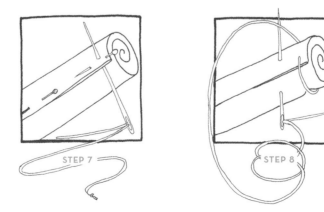

STEP 7   STEP 8

4. Fold the short ends of your rectangle in toward the center. The ends should butt up against each other but not overlap. If you are using a cut sleeve tube, center the seam. Gently smooth in place.

5. Beginning at one cut end, roll the leg into a log shape and pin in place. Check to be sure that the folded edges are at the top and bottom of your log shape. (If you are using a cut-sleeve piece, begin at one short cut edge and roll tightly.)

6. Pin the rolled edge in place.

7. Hold the rolled and pinned leg log so the cut edge is horizontal and facing you. Insert threaded needle ½" under the top layer at the corner and pull through to the knot. This will conceal the knot under the top layer of fabric.

8. With a firm grip and creating a little tension, wrap the yarn toward your body, move the yarn down around the bottom of the log shape, all the way around, past the cut edge, ending up just below where you started. Maintain the tension on the yarn by holding it securely in place with your thumb. Insert the needle below the cut edge and make it come out equidistantly above the cut edge; pull the needle away from you and all the way through.

9. Continue on with this technique, wrapping toward you and stitching away, traveling ½" to 1" toward the end of the log each time you wrap. When you get ¾" from the bottom, stop.

10. Now you are going to change the direction of wrapping. With a firm grip on the yarn, begin wrapping with tension all the way back to the top where you began. Poke your needle straight through the leg log and pull your yarn through. Tie a simple overhand knot next to the surface of the fabric. Poke the needle back through the leg, pull yarn through, and cut it off flush with the surface of the fabric.

11. At the end opposite the knots, cut "toes" by curling back the outer layer of fabric and making five snips no deeper than ½" around the circumference.

12. Fold all these toes back and cut off the inner layers of the log, making the toes flare out and enabling the leg to stand (with luck).

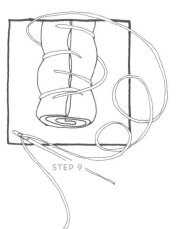

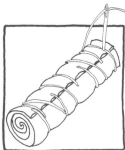

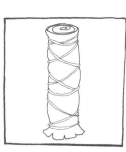

STEP 9   STEP 10   STEP 11   STEP 12

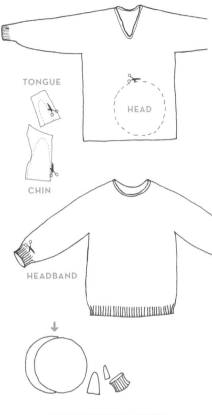

TONGUE

CHIN

HEADBAND

SAMPLE CUTTING LAYOUT

RAGAMUFFIN HEAD

The Ragamuffin head (the same for all Ragamuffins) is made of several parts: head piece, chin, tongue, and a headband. For the main head piece, you should use a thick, heavily felted wool fabric; texture is more important than color here. If the fabric you want to use is not very firm, you can stack two pieces of a thinner felt (or even just an extra half) and use them as one. It is important to have sturdy bulk to make a nice head, otherwise it may come out thin, floppy, and insubstantial. The chin should be cut from a dense midweight felt in any color other than red or pink. Why? Because you should use a pink or red thin, fine knit wool for the tongue. For the headband, choose a felted sweater cuff; although any one will work fine, interesting details such as stripes, unique ribbing, or extra length add a lot to this piece.

CUTTING THE PIECES

1. For the main head piece, trace around a 10" dinner plate or other circular object with a felt-tip marker on heavy, thick felted fabric. With fabric scissors, cut it out, and then snip triangles about 1" apart, all the way around the circle's circumference.

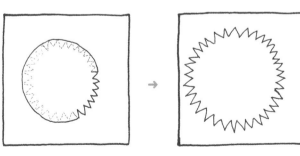

STEP 1

2. For the chin, cut an arch shape about 2½" tall in the center and 2" at the base.

3. For the tongue, cut a tall, narrow arch shape about 2" long at longest point and ¾" wide, cut from thin, finely knit, felted wool in red or pink.

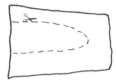

STEP 3

4. For the headband, use a sweater cuff with nice details; a plain brightly colored cuff works just fine too.

SEWING

Forming the Main Head Piece

5. Fold the cut head piece in half just slightly off-center so that one zig-zagged edge lays just inside the other. Work with this side up so you can see it.

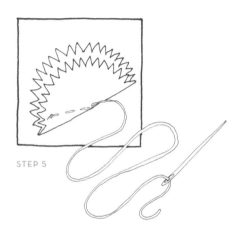

STEP 5

Thread your needle with a full strand of sewing yarn about 1½ yards long. With a long, quick running stitch and beginning 2" from the zig-zagged edge, baste toward the center of the fold. The folded head piece will be held in place with these big basting stitches. Leave your needle threaded, with the yarn hanging out of the middle of the flat edge of the semicircle.

6. Roll this semicircle into a tight cone shape, beginning at one side and rolling toward the other, hiding your basting stitches inside the roll. Keep the center of the straight, folded side pointy, with the yarn hanging out from the point. Hold cone roll intact with your thumb stuck right into the center of the cone and your index finger holding the outside end firmly.

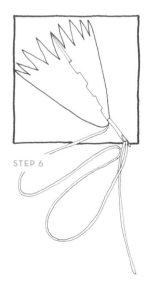

STEP 6

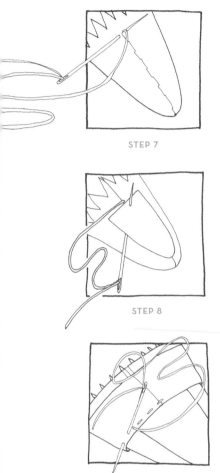

STEP 7

STEP 8

With the threaded needle, begin ½" in from the very tip of the point and blind stitch toward the wide end, being sure to hold the cone roll tight.

7. Stop stitching when you get about 1½" from the zigzagged edge. Pull yarn tight to round the pointy end and make it more noselike. Secure this roundedness with a double stitch.

Attaching the Chin

8. Poke your needle through the middle of the flat edge of the chin piece, about ¼" in from the edge. Pull your yarn through and center chin piece over the blind-stitched seam to conceal it.

Attaching the Headband

9. Fold the headband in half as though you were folding up your sleeve. Pull it around the cone, with the folded edge toward the narrower (nose) end. Swivel the headband around to be sure the seam is lined up with the middle of the bottom of the chin. Stick your needle through the headband either into or right next to the seam. Carefully holding the headband to cover the flat edge of the chin, running stitch the headband in place, being sure you are going through the chin, both layers of cuff, and at least one layer of the head piece. Stitch all the way around, staying about ¼" in from the folded edge of the headband. Make your stitches small enough to keep little kid fingers from being able to get under them easily.

STEP 9

Completing the Chin and Tongue

10. When you get back to where you started, stick your needle in, making the last stitch of the headband, and bring it out at the corner of the chin piece and the headband.

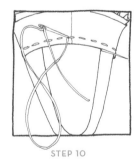

STEP 10

11. Whip stitch one side of the chin in place, from the folded cuff edge toward the nose, with four or five stitches.

12. Insert tongue piece, flat edge in, between chin and head. Stick the needle in the beginning of the last stitch you took, poke it through the tongue with an "in and out," and finally have the needle come out, making the first stitch through the other side of the chin.

13. Beginning with a double stitch to make the sides look even, whip stitch the other side of the chin in place with four or five stitches (matching the other side), working toward the headband.

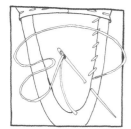

STEP 11

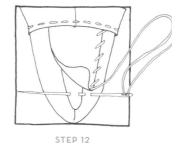

STEP 12

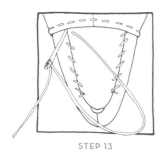

STEP 13

CRISPINA'S
DESIGN NOTES

A fun challenge is to save all your scraps and see how many you can use. While some of the projects in this book use small bits, there are always leftovers to be alchemized. For instance, save all the scrap seams, knot them end-to-end, and you've got festive gift ribbon that even looks super-cool just sitting in a ball on the coffee table.

safety first

The button eyes used on the Ragamuffin head may not be safe for children under the age of three. If a small one will have access to your stuffed creation, you can embroider simple eyes with colorful yarn or thread instead.

FINISHING TOUCHES

14. When you get back to the headband, stick the needle straight through the head and come out where you would like the first eye to be. Stitch a small button in place using three or four repeated stitches, being sure to pull tightly as you go. Dip the needle back through, coming out where you would like the second eye. Stitch that one on in the same way as the first.

15. Insert the needle all the way back through the head, coming out at the very bottom in the headband. Tie a knot close to the surface of the fabric, conceal your end, and snip off the yarn flush with the cloth.

16. Make cuts about 2" long all around the headband, using the ribbing as a guide. Don't cut into the running stitches.

Yay! Your head is done — you've just finished the hardest part. Congratulations!

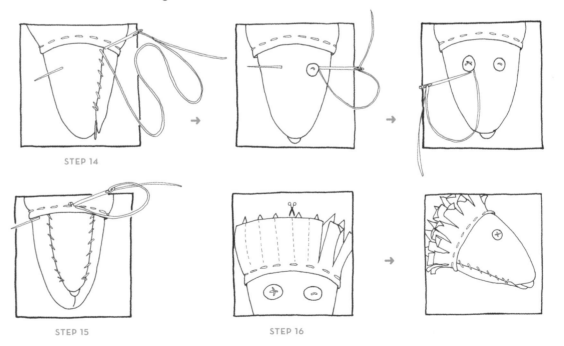

STEP 14

STEP 15   STEP 16

head piece

Long Leg piece

tongue

Ragamuffin head: the same for all three styles

Stand-up 't-shirt'

Pot Belly Body

tail: the same for all three styles

Chin

Dinosaur Body piece

Neck cuff

Short leg: Dino only

Short leg piece #1

Stuffing

Short leg piece #2

DINOSAUR
RAGAMUFFIN BODY

The first hand-felted Ragamuffins I made morphed into this style, which I came to call a dinosaur, since there was a dinosaur fad taking the land by storm at the time. So here you go — off to make a creature that you have the luxury to name on your own or call a Dinosaur.

you will need

» Ruler
» 10" square of felted wool for the Dino body
» Sharp fabric scissors
» A size 18 yarn darner needle
» Persian wool sewing yarn in several different colors
» Extra-long straight pins
» Completed Ragamuffin Tail (see page 114)
» Ribbing cut from the bottom of a thick, well-felted sweater for back spine, approximately 2½" wide and 12" long without seams (*Note:* The ribbing from one sweater usually yields two spines. It is possible to use thinner, softer fabric if you don't mind the spine flopping over one side or the other.)

» Stuffing material (this can be tiny bits of scrap from the project, wool fleece, or, in a pinch, polyester fiberfill)
» Completed Ragamuffin Head (see pages 118–122)
» Two pairs of Completed Ragamuffin Short Legs (see pages 115–117); can be two different lengths

optional

» Flattened cereal box
» Permanent felt-tip marker
» Household scissors
» Small spring-loaded pliers

124

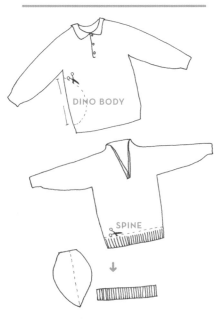

DINO BODY

SPINE

SAMPLE CUTTING LAYOUT

STEP 2

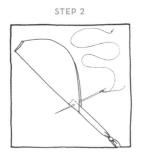

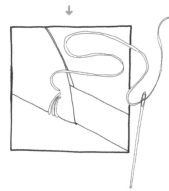

PREPARING YOUR MATERIALS

To make a Dinosaur, you'll need a completed head, tail, and four short legs. You will also need to make a Dino body. In choosing the appropriate felted fabric for the body, remember that color, texture, or pattern should play an important part. Stretchy felt will make a fatter body, while denser, less elastic material allows for a leaner, less squishy body. In any case, do not use felted wool made from very loose or large gauge knits or the stuffing may show.

CUTTING AND SEWING THE DINO BODY

Cutting the Dino Body and Spine

1. Using the cutting layout drawing at left as a guide, cut a teardrop-shaped Dino body, 9" long, from a square of processed felt. It is easy to cut this piece freehand on the fold, pointed at one end and curving wide and finishing with a flat end. (As an alternative, make a pattern using the cereal box. Cut out the pattern with household scissors, and trace around it using the felt-tip marker on the processed fabric. Remember to cut inside the marker line so that it does not show on the cut fabric.) Cut off a bottom ribbing piece for the spine.

Attaching the Tail

2. Thread the needle with a yard of sewing yarn. With Dino body folded in half wrong sides together, place tail between layers at the pointed end of the body piece. Insert the threaded needle between the Dino body layers, tacking the tail in place to begin sewing.

3. Bring your needle and sewing yarn to the outside of the Dino body and stitch tail in place, sewing through all layers with three strong stitches, pulling yarn tight as you go. Leave the needle with yarn attached for the next step.

Attaching the Spine

4. Insert about 1" of the cut edge of the spine between the layers of the Dino body, carefully following the back shape and allowing the spine to curve. It will likely flop over in one direction or the other, which is okay. Pin in place.

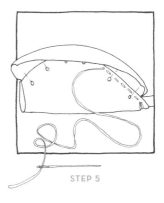

STEP 5

5. With a small running stitch, sew from tail end toward flat end, carefully going through both sides of the Dino body with the spine between. Try to keep the Dino body piece even on either side of the spine. When you get to the flat end, leave needle threaded and dangling and stop sewing.

6. Snip spine into 1" to 2" wide fringe.

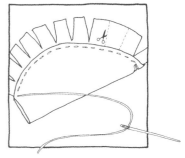

STEP 6

Finishing the Body

7. Stuff the Dino body. Be sure to get right down into the point at the tail end. (I find an unsharpened pencil is handy for getting into the smallest areas.) Stuff evenly and firmly.

   Your sewing yarn might have opened up a bit in the stuffing process so pull it snug, being careful not to pucker the fabric or leave your stitches too loose. Make an in-place stitch to secure the running stitches. Leave a yarn end to use for securing the Dinosaur head to the body.

CONSTRUCTING THE DINOSAUR

Attaching the Head to the Dino Body

8. Sit in a chair and hold the Dino body between your legs with the spine facing up. Thread the existing yarn from the Dino body on your needle.

   Line up the head with the Dino body. Be sure the chin is evenly aligned with the bottom of the Dino body and the spine is aligned with the space between the eyes. You will be blind stitching the head

STEP 8

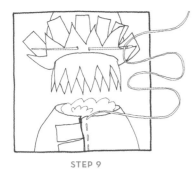

STEP 9

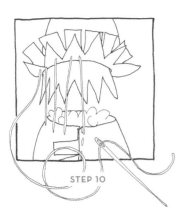

STEP 10

to the Dino body; all but a single layer of the pointed "dreadlocks" of the Dino head will be stuffed inside the opening of the Dino body. Hold the top layer of points of the Ragamuffin head down over the eyes so that you can best see what you are doing. Your blind stitches will alternate between the back of this top layer of zigzag points and the stuffed Dino body.

9.   Begin with a horizontal stitch about ½" in length in the top layer of zigzag points. The material should be thick enough to take a stitch without going all the way through the fabric (keeping the "blind" in blind stitch).

10. Your second stitch will go into the Dino body about ¾" in from the cut edge, again about ½" in length and running horizontally. (The ¾" seam allowance here will fold under as you work and be tucked inside the Dino body along with the head points.) Then go back into the head material with ½" between this and the last stitch in the head. It is easiest to keep these stitches loose. Continue in this manner until you are halfway around the head and body. Your yarn will begin to look like a ladder between the head and body.

Note: To arrive halfway around the head *and* halfway around the body with the same stitch will likely require some easing. Adjust your stitches as needed to make this happen.

As you move around to the bottom of the Dino body, increase the distance between the cut edge of the Dino body and your stitches to make the head look down. There is a lot of manipulation possible here. You can experiment. There will be a place at the bottom of the head where the cone roll has a blind-stitched seam. At this point, poke your needle through the seam from one side to the other, return to a stitch in the head, and so on. Gently pull the yarn tight, closing up the ladder gap and making stitches tight. Be careful not to break the yarn.

Insert the zigzagged points of the head into the hole in the Dino body and sew second part of head seam.

11. When you get back to where you started, *carefully* pull the yarn tight a second time. This should make the head attach securely to the body with no stitches visible. Take a couple more stitches, overlapping with the first few you took.

12. Poke the needle through to end at a place you would like to sew on a front leg.

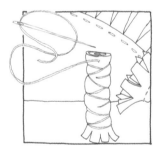

Attaching the Front Legs

13. Using one of the shorter of the two pairs of legs you have made, poke the needle straight through the leg, about ½" down from the top. Pull your yarn through, positioning the leg to lay flat on the surface of the Dino body.

14. Wrap the yarn over the top of the leg, stitching deep into the Dino body and coming out in the same place you did with your last stitch. You may need to use a small pair of pliers to pull the needle and yarn through so many layers of cloth. Repeat this step two more times, pulling the yarn tight between each stitch.

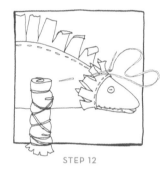

15. Now wrap the yarn around the back side of the leg, taking the same deep stitch into the stuffing and back through the leg; repeat. Do the same to the front side of the leg (see step 17 detail illustration on next page). Tie a knot close to the surface of the fabric, then poke your needle back down into the fabric, exiting an inch or two away. Snip off the yarn flush with the surface of the fabric.

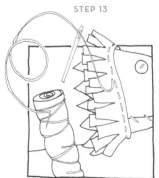

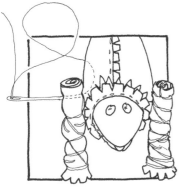

STEP 16

STEP 17

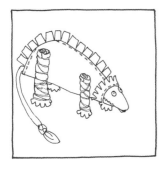

STEP 18

16. Hold the second leg of the shorter pair on the other side of the Dino body, lining up the feet so they are level. The top of the leg has a little leeway, but the feet should be made even so that your Dino will stand when completed. Begin sewing by running your needle straight through the leg about 1" down from the top. Then hold the leg in place against the Dino body, concealing the knot.

17. Wrap the sewing yarn over the top of the leg, stitch deep into the stuffing, and pop your needle back out where your first stitch came out of the leg. Repeat to have three stitches over the top of the leg and two stitches over either side. Remember to pull the yarn taut between stitches.

Finish by tying a knot close to the surface, then poke needle back into fabric, exiting an inch or two away, and snip yarn flush with fabric.

Attaching the Back Legs

18. The back legs are attached in the same manner. They, too, should be lined up evenly with the feet of the front legs in order to make the finished Dinosaur stand. Hips (the top of the rear legs) can fall anywhere on the Dino body and can be quite high up.

When you have the second of the rear legs attached, you are done!

Congratulations! You have finished a Dinosaur Ragamuffin!

EYEGLASSES CASE

This useful scrap project can be made to fit whatever you need to hold, whether it's eyeglasses, an MP3 player, or some other gadget requiring a case. Simply fold a piece of scrap cloth over your glasses, or the object you want it to hold, to get a general sense of the required size. Allowing enough extra material for a ½" seam allowance, cut the scrap into a tidy rectangle. Leaving the short end open, running stitch the other sides together. I've added a densely felted strip attached to the back, cut long enough to fold over the open top of the case and button on the front.

Make the tab fit neatly to hold in contents.

Cut a short snip for a buttonhole so button fits snugly.

POTBELLY
RAGAMUFFIN BODY

All the Ragamuffins are cute, but Potbellies are *really* cute. While the other style Ragamuffins seem to appeal more to kids, Potbellies tend to appeal to adults who want to display a little bit of crazy humor and whimsy in an otherwise serious setting. Potbellies allow people to live vicariously through them, inspiring a kind of mischief.

you will need

» One 3½" to 4" circle of thick and firm felted wool (the top of a large coffee cup or sour cream container would work well for a pattern)

» One 8" circle of thin and stretchy felted wool (try a dessert plate to trace for this pattern)

» A size 18 yarn darner needle

» Persian wool in several colors

» Stuffing material (this can be tiny bits of scrap from the project, wool fleece, or, in a pinch, polyester fiberfill)

» Completed Ragamuffin Head (see pages 118–122)

» Completed Ragamuffin Tail (see page 114)

optional

» Small spring-loaded pliers

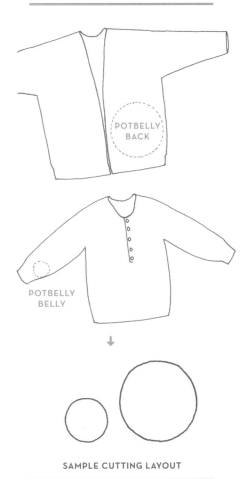

POTBELLY
BACK

POTBELLY
BELLY

SAMPLE CUTTING LAYOUT

PREPARING YOUR MATERIALS

To make a Potbelly you will again need a completed head, tail, and four short legs. The body consists of two circles: The smaller 4" circle (the belly) should be cut from fairly thick and dense fabric, but the larger 8" circle (the back) needs to be a thin and stretchy finely knit cloth, as it will have to be gathered during construction. Again, color and pattern can be an important component in making this funny little creature.

SEWING THE POTBELLY BODY

1. Thread your needle with a yard of Persian wool, knotted at one end. Insert the needle through the 4" circle from back to front about ¼" from the edge.

2. Hold the 4" circle edge next to the 8" circle, edge to edge, with the knot between them. Tack together by making an in-place stitch through both pieces.

3. With the larger circle on top, begin sewing the circles together with a running stitch, pinching and pleating the 8" circle each time and securing that gather as you stitch. Check the circles from one side to the other with each stitch to make sure stitch placement and length are even. Keep the edges flush as you work your way around.

STEP 2

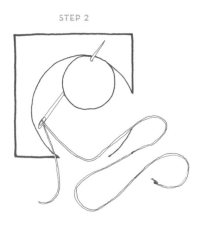

STEP 3

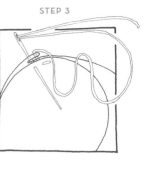

4. When you run out of excess material to gather from the 8" circle, stuff the Potbelly body. Be sure to get an even and firm finish.

5. Finish the seam with a small running stitch, securing the stuffing inside. Make an in-place stitch, knot off, and conceal end.

CONSTRUCTING THE POTBELLY

Attaching the Head to the Body

6. Thread a needle with 1½ yards of sewing yarn and knot one end. Hold the Potbelly body in your hand with the small circle facing you. Hold the head in place over the nongathered part of the seam around the 4" circle on the Potbelly body. Make a small stitch in the chin. Realign the head and body, concealing the knot in the chin.

7. Sew a large, deep, horizontal stitch (about 1½") across the top of the Potbelly body, right under the head. Keeping the head and body matched, make a large horizontal stitch clear across the chin, sewing as deep into the head as you can. Pull the stitch tight. Repeat twice, so your last stitch exists where you would like the first "arm" to be.

Attaching the First Arm

8. Using one of the shorter pairs of legs, poke the needle straight through the leg about 1" down from the top. Pull your yarn through, positioning the arm/leg to lay flat on the surface of the Potbelly body. Position the arm the way you would like it by holding it firmly next to the body. Wrap the yarn over the top of the arm, stitching deep into the Potbelly body and coming out in the same place you did with your last stitch. A small pair of pliers to pull the needle and yarn through so many layers of cloth makes this job a lot easier. Repeat this step two more times, pulling the yarn tight between each stitch. Now, wrap the yarn over the left side of the arm, making a deep stitch into the stuffing and coming back up through the arm where your last stitch exited. Repeat. Finally, do the same to the right side of the arm.

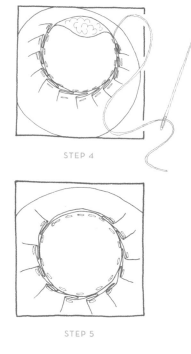

STEP 4

STEP 5

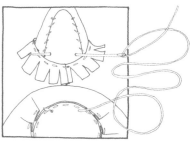

STEP 6

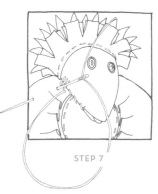

STEP 7

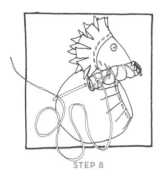

STEP 8

STEP 10

STEP 11

Tie a knot close to the surface of the fabric, then poke your needle back down into the fabric, exiting an inch or two away. Snip off the yarn flush with the surface of the fabric.

Attaching the Second Arm

9. Hold the second of the shorter pair of arms/legs on the other side of the Potbelly body where you would like it attached. Sew the second arm on in the same way as the first. Begin by running your needle straight through the arm about 1" down from the top. Then hold the arm in place against the Potbelly body, concealing the knot. Wrap the sewing yarn over the top of the arm, stitch deep into the stuffing, and pop your needle back out where your first stitch exited. Repeat to have three stitches over the top of the arm and two stitches over either side. Remember to pull the yarn taut between stitches. Cut, knot, and conceal yarn.

Attaching the Legs

10. The legs are set in a sort of triangle to enable the Potbelly to sit up. Imagine the tops of the legs pretty close together yet angled away from each other, forming a three-pointed base for the Potbelly to balance on. Each leg forms one of the three points and the bottom of the belly makes the third. Stitch on the legs as you did the arms.

11. Once you have the legs sewn in place, center the tail between them and stitch that down with the same technique. Yea! You are done!

for secure attachments

When attaching any short leg or tail to a Raga-muffin, there are three strong, tight stitches over the top, and two strong, tight stitches over either side of the appendage you are adding. With this extra touch, everything should stay in place.

FINGER PUPPETS

These are really fun, expressive little things! They're quick and easy to make from the smallest scraps around. I like to make them fit the fingers they will sit on. Pictured here are some simple ideas to get you started. If the right buttons are not available, use tiny bits of cloth with a small stitch in the middle for eyes. Add wings and feet or stay simple. Make a handful!

STAND-UP
RAGAMUFFIN BODY

Stand-up Ragamuffins are the favorite style for kids who love to take care of "babies." The construction of the Stand-up Ragamuffin differs from the other two; it is derived from the process, as it was explained to me, used to make traditional corn husk dolls. It still uses the same head and tail as the others, but the body is made by combining two long legs. The long legs can be different sizes and thicknesses. If you are using stretchy or not well-felted cloth, be sure to cut the toes and fingers really small so they stay secure and do not pull off.

you will need

» 2 adult-size felted pullover sweaters (see pages 20–21), at least 16" across from side seam to side seam
» Measuring tape
» Sharp fabric scissors
» A size 18 yarn darner needle
» Persian wool in several colors

» Extra-long straight pins
» A 6" x 14" brightly colored or interestingly patterned felted wool scrap for Stand-up clothing (T-shirt)
» Completed Ragamuffin Head (see pages 118–122)
» Completed Ragamuffin Tail (see page 114)

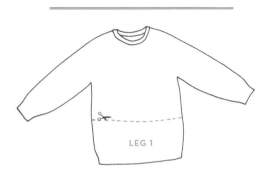

LEG 1

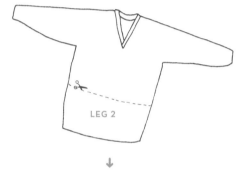

LEG 2

SAMPLE CUTTING LAYOUT

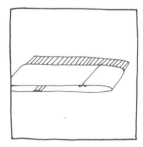

STEP 3

PREPARING YOUR MATERIALS

All of the guidelines for making Short Legs (see pages 115–117) also apply to Long Legs. Texture is fine; loosely or open-knit fabrics aren't. Remember that you will be sewing through many layers, so I don't recommend a very heavy, dense felt.

Long legs should be at least 14" long when complete, so extra small or kid-size sweaters are not useful for making these pieces.

CUTTING AND CONSTRUCTING THE LONG LEGS

Cutting the Long Leg

1. For each long leg (you will make two for the Stand-up Ragamuffin), cut a large rectangle of double thickness straight across the body of a felted pullover sweater. This piece should be anywhere from 5" to 7" wide and as long as the width of the sweater. To make a long leg about 14" (the optimal length), it is best to start with a piece cut 14" to 18" long.

Constructing the Long Leg

2. Thread your needle with a piece of yarn about 3 yards long. Tie a knot in one end and return it to your pincushion.

3. Refold the tube you cut for this piece by moving any seams away from the ends. There are usually two seams, one from either side of the sweater body. These should not be at the very sides where snipping toes (after construction) could cause a problem, and they should not be overlapping in the middle of the piece where they could make a fat lump.

4. Beginning at one long side with cut edges, tightly roll the cloth into an extra long log shape and pin in place. As you roll, pull the outer layer toward the far end, being sure that you are rolling and pinning evenly

and aren't going to end up with a large blob of extra cloth sticking out of the center when you get to the end. This might take a few tries.

5. Hold the rolled and pinned long-leg log so the cut edge is horizontal and facing you. About ¾" from one end, insert needle ½" in from the cut edge under top layer, and pull through to the knot. This will conceal the knot under the top layer of fabric.

6. Hold the yarn about 8" from where it is coming out of the felted fabric, and with a firm grip to create a little tension, wrap the yarn toward you, all the way around the log, past the cut edge, ending up just beyond where you started. With your thumb, hold yarn in place, maintaining tightness. Insert needle ½" below the cut edge, come out equidistant above the cut edge, and pull the needle away from you, extending the full length of yarn, and tug for tightness. Continue on with this technique, wrapping toward you and stitching away each time you wrap traveling ½" to 1" toward the end of the log. When you get ¾" from the end, stop.

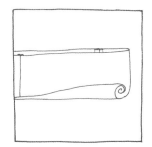

STEP 4

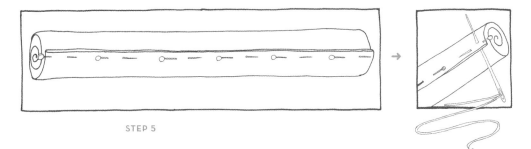

STEP 5

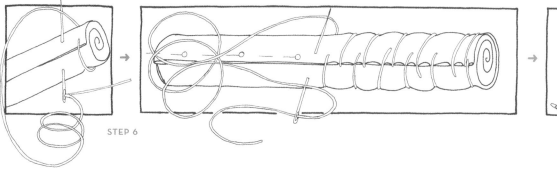

STEP 6

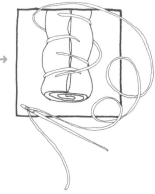

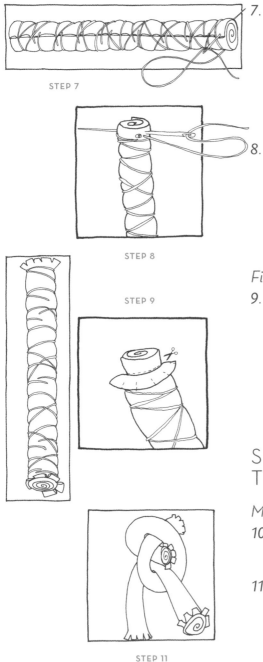

STEP 7

STEP 8

STEP 9

STEP 11

7. Now you are going to change the direction of wrapping. With a firm grip on the yarn, begin wrapping with a bit of tension all the way back to the end where you began. On the return wrapping there are no stitches between wraps. You will likely run out of yarn. It is fine to add to your yarn with a simple overhand knot — leave tails a couple of inches long so they are easier to hide later.

8. When you get back to the end where you started, poke your needle straight through the leg and pull your yarn through. Tie a simple over-hand knot next to the surface of the fabric.

   Poke the needle back through the leg next to the knot, pull your yarn through, and cut it off flush with the surface of the leg.

Finishing the Long Leg

9. Long legs have "toes" at both ends. Cut them by folding back the outer layer of the roll and making five small snips around the circum-ference, no deeper than ½". Fold all these toes back and cut out the center of the log to make the toes flare out, creating a palmlike detail. Do this on both ends of your long leg.

   Repeat to make a second long leg.

SEWING AND CONSTRUCTING THE STAND-UP RAGAMUFFIN

Making the Body

10. Thread a needle with 1½ yards of sewing yarn and knot at one end. Set aside.

11. Make the Stand-up body by tying two Long Legs together with a sim-ple, very loose overhand knot in the thinner leg. Thread the thicker leg through the hole in the knot. Pull the overhand knot as tight as you can, securing the legs together. This makes the body of this Raga-muffin: One long leg becomes the legs, the other becomes the arms.

If the arms seem too long, you can tie a second knot with them, shortening them a bit.

Attaching the Head

12. Center the head on top of the knot created by the Long Leg that will be the arms. With the threaded needle, take a small stitch in the Ragamuffin head. Realign the head and body, concealing the knot in the chin and centering the head.

STEP 12

13. Make a large, deep horizontal stitch about 1½" across the top of the leg knot right under the head. (Be sure you are sewing through both sides of the knot to keep it intact and tight). Keeping the head and body together, take another large horizontal stitch across the chin, sewing as deeply into the head as you can. Pull the stitch tight. Repeat twice more, pulling the yarn tightly after each stitch, exiting where you can knot and cut the yarn so that it will be covered by the T-shirt.

STEP 13

Dressing the Stand-up

14. Fold the T-shirt rectangle in half so it is squarish. Carefully snip a hole in the middle of the fold to make a little poncholike piece.

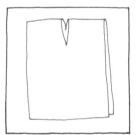

STEP 14

15. Pull the T-shirt down over the Ragamuffin Head. Snip it open more in the front if necessary. Match up the front and back corners on one side. Begin stitching by poking the needle through one side of the fabric from the inside to the outside. Rematch the corners, concealing the knot. Wrap the yarn around the bottom edge of the matched-up corners and, using a very small running stitch, sew through both layers from hem edge to armpit. Just before you reach the armpit, stop. Wrap the yarn around the outside of both layers and stitch back through them both. Make a knot close to the surface, conceal the end, and snip off the extra yarn. Sew up the other side in the same way.

STEP 15

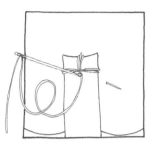

STEP 16

STEP 17

16. Sew a running stitch between the legs: Begin by inserting the threaded needle at the bottom from the wrong side of either the front or back (so that the knot is concealed). Wrap the yarn around the bottom edge of the fabric and come straight through, joining front to back. Using a small running stitch, continue to join the front and back of the T-shirt between the Ragamuffin's legs until you get to the Long Leg knot on the inside. Exit through the knot, coming out on the back of the Ragamuffin where you want to place the tail.

17. Push the needle through the middle of the tail about ½" from the short flat edge. Wrap the yarn over the top of the tail, stitching deep into the Stand-up knot. Repeat this stitch twice more. Now wrap the yarn around one side of the tail in the same fashion as you did the short flat edge. Stitch twice around each side. Finish by tying a knot close to the surface of the fabric, concealing the end, and snipping off extra yarn.

   Yay! You are done.

CHAPTER 7

FESTIVE SCRAP PROJECTS

This is a great chapter for people, like myself, who are
DRIVEN TO USE EVERY LITTLE LAST BIT OF MATERIAL

rather than return it on its journey to the landfill, or for beginners who want to try out a few projects without a big time commitment. The simple projects in this chapter make especially great gifts for special occasions or decorations for seasonal celebrations. Wreaths and flowers require no sewing skills at all. The small sewing projects in this chapter make a nice way to introduce new sewers, including children, to the whimsy and fun of this type of crafting.

When the production company I ran was in full swing, we offered free bags of scrap at the door of both our retail shop and the studio. The inspiration that grew out of these bags was amazing. There were bed-sized blankets painstakingly hand sewn from tiny bits with great detail. A high school teacher engaged her students in a year long assignment creating a group blanket. The Garden Flowers (see pages 152–157) were inspired by a scrap user. Wreaths and bobbles were designed specifically to make more efficient use of our raw material in the studio. It was my intention to have a show of the truly remarkable stuff people came up with all made from scrap. Maybe that can still happen — so use this chapter to launch you into the wild world of obsessive recycling paired with right brain nirvana and let's see what unfolds. And don't forget, when all else fails, you can use little pieces for Ragamuffin or Pillow stuffing.

You will find a couple more fun scrap projects on pages 131 and 137.

BUSINESS CARD CASE

To make your one-of-a-kind card holder, start with a stack of business cards, traditionally 2"×3.5". Cut a rectangle ¾" wider than the cards and almost three times the width of the cards. Fold the cloth around the cards and stitch up the sides with a running stich. Decoratively edge the flap of the case with blanket stitch. If the cloth is heavily felted, you can make tiny slits for buttonholes. If the cloth is looser knit, it's best to use Velcro or snap tape for the closure, and add decorative buttons just for flair.

BABY CHICKS

Felt chicks are cute, simple little things that add flare to your spring decorating. They are super cute placed in an egg carton for a spring centerpiece. They are also fun to carry in your pocket as "worry dolls." I have also customized the design to make finger puppets for my kids. They are an easy beginner's project for children interested in hand-sewing projects.

When selecting material for these, I try to find the fuzziest, softest, most baby-chick-colored yellow I can. The orange material should be stable and not ravelly.

you will need

» Scraps of well-felted yellow and orange wool sweaters

» Sharp fabric scissors

» A size 14 yarn darner needle

» Yellow Persian wool yarn

» Stuffing material (I prefer raw wool, although you can use scraps of felted fabric that have been finely cut into small bits or even polyester fiberfill)

» Two small, flat, 2- or 4-hole buttons for eyes (be sure your threaded needle fits through the holes)

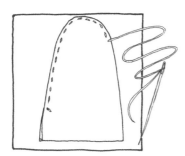

STEP 4

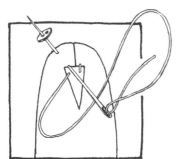

STEP 6

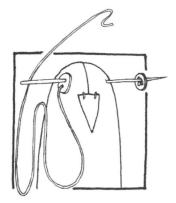

STEP 7

PREPARING YOUR MATERIALS

1. Cut an arch shape on the fold of the yellow felted fabric. The arch should be 3½" to 4" tall at center and 2½" wide at bottom of flat edge. When it is open it should look like a big, yellow, filled-in M. (Chicken nuggets anyone?)

2. Cut three little orange triangles, two for the feet and one for the beak.

SEWING

3. Thread the needle with a yard of yellow sewing yarn.

4. With the yellow fabric folded right sides together, begin stitching ¾" up from the bottom on the open side. Wrap your first stitch around the side before continuing up, and wrap the yarn around the top curve with a tiny running stitch. End with a stitch in place. Poke your needle through to the inside of the shape at the end of your seam.

5. With needle and yarn still attached, turn the chick right side out. Stuff the chick's body firmly, leaving the bottom ¾" empty.

6. Center the beak over the end of the seam and tack in place at each corner with two small, tidy stitches. Emerge from the last beak stitch where you would like an eye to be.

7. Sew on each button eye with two stitches. Emerge from the last eye stitch down through the open bottom.

8. Close the fabric at the bottom like the end of a gift-wrapped package, folding the front toward the back and then both sides toward the middle, overlapping neatly. Stitch this fold in place with a tidy small whip stitch.

9. Tack the feet in place with a generously sized stitch in the center of each foot. Emerge from foot stitches at crown of head, just above the eyes. Knot close to the surface of the fabric. Leave a ½" tuft and snip off extra yarn.

10. Pull the excess fabric to the back, forming a cute little tail. Stitch across the tail to secure stuffing inside. Fluff tuft to make a head feather. HOW CUTE!

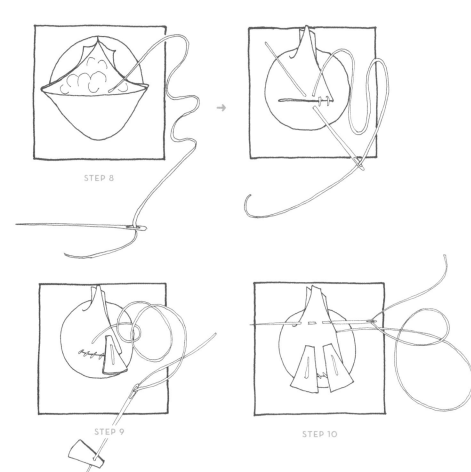

STEP 8

STEP 9

STEP 10

GARDEN FLOWERS

The basic technique for making flowers is so simple that children can easily do it. However, the technique also can be highly refined and detailed for those who relish that type of work. I will begin by explaining the simplest technique to get you started. Once you understand the basics you can use your own creativity or some of the variations I'll spell out for more complicated and intricate items. These look best in a bunch, so plan to make at least a dozen of them.

you will need

» Ruler
» A pair of wire cutters
» 8 yards of 20-gauge galvanized steel wire
» Scraps of various floral-colored felted wool knits from other projects
» Sharp fabric scissors or a rotary cutter and pad
» A handful of assorted buttons
» 12 narrow strips of green fabric or green seam binding, 16" long
» White craft glue

optional

» An electric drill
» 24-gauge galvanized steel wire (see Flower Variations)
» Small spring-loaded pliers

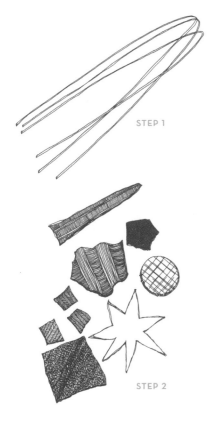

STEP 1

STEP 2

STEP 6

PREPARING YOUR MATERIALS

1. Measure and cut 12 pieces of wire, each about 24" long. Bend wire lengths in half, making the ends even. Do not crease the wire.

2. Cut scraps of fabric into squares, circles, triangles, and strips of varying sizes. Shapes can range from ½" across to 2½" or even 3" across if the fabric has enough body to hold itself without looking floppy or wilted. Strips are best cut from thin cloth without much body and are useful up to 6" in length and 1" wide. You will need about 36 individual cut pieces to make a dozen flowers, more if possible. Flowers look really good with at least three different fabrics. Bright shades of natural flower colors are my favorite.

3. Using the cut pieces of scrap, make 12 stacks that will become your flower petals. Start each stack with bigger pieces and pile on three or four pieces of decreasing size. Pay attention to color combinations and how your shapes work together to create a flowerlike appearance.

4. Build a stack of two or three buttons that coordinate well with each stack of petals. You will want to make the piles of buttons start with the biggest and work toward the smallest. Flat buttons with either two or four holes work best for this, although shank buttons are fine for the top of the stack. Shank buttons also look nice threaded next to each other and manipulated to all face up in bunches.

CONSTRUCTING THE FLOWERS

5. Even the ends of the wire with wire cutters if necessary.

6. Slip buttons onto both wire ends, threading each end through a hole in each flat button, or just through the shank on shank buttons. Pull the stack of buttons to the very middle of the fold in the wire. Occasionally, if the buttons are especially small or if the stack of buttons

is especially tall, it can be difficult to pull the buttons to the center of the wire. If this is the case, use your hands or a pair of small pliers to manipulate the wire and make it easier to pull them to the center.

7. With the smallest pieces on top, pick up a whole stack of the scrap arranged into petals. Hold the wires near the bottom with your other hand. With the two wire ends about ½" apart, apply gentle pressure to the top of the stack of fabric. Wiggle the wires back and forth, keeping pressure even; slowly but surely the wire ends will work themselves into and then through the stack, top to bottom. Push the stack to the center fold of the wire to meet the buttons.

8. Thread a strip of green fabric onto one of the wires and slide it to meet the scraps.

9. Twist together the two ends of the wire either by hand, or by inserting the ends into an electric drill with the bit removed. Tighten drill closed around the wires. While holding the flower head and fabric tightly against the buttons with one hand, gently spin the wires to twist just enough to hold the petals firmly in place. Be careful not to over twist or the wires will curl up on themselves like old telephone cords.

10. Wrap the wire stem with the strip of green fabric fastened in the wire twist: Hold the ribbon flat, angled toward the bottom of the stem, between your thumb and forefinger. Spin the wire with your other hand and let the ribbon pull through your fingers with a little tension. Move along the stem to cover the length with an inch or two of green ribbon to spare. When you get to the bottom, fold the ribbon back onto the stem while continuing to spin the stem in the same direction. When the ribbon is too small to hold onto, put a little dab of white glue on the inside of the ribbon end and press it down smoothly.

TA-DA! You are done with your first flower!

designer stacking tips

* *Strips can be used alone or stacked with other shapes.*

* *Longer strips can be folded, accordion-style, to make a ruffled rose-shaped flower.*

* *I often add a small leaf-shaped piece of green to the bottom of the stack, transitioning the colorful petals to stem with an element of reality.*

STEP 7

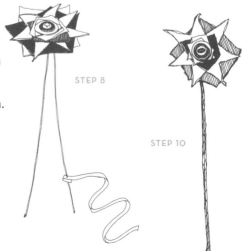

STEP 8

STEP 10

FLOWER VARIATIONS

» *Make many small flowers* using 24-gauge wire and wrap them all onto one stem to create spire-shaped hyacinths or delphinium blooms. Wrap the small stems together using an additional length of 24-gauge wire. Finish the stem with a wrap of ribbon or green cloth strips, as above.

» *Cut leaf shapes* and add them to one side of the wire before you twist the stem. To give leaves more body, they can be made with a wire support "stitched" into each leaf's center line. Use a folded length of 24-gauge wire inserted into the leaf by accordion-folding the fabric and poking the points through.

» *Make tall stamens.* Using fine wire, thread a button on to each of three or four 4"–6" lengths folded in half. Twist each thin wire a few times by hand, keeping the twist right next to the button. When the twist reaches about 1" in length, spin all the stamens into one bunch. Snip off excess wire. Or begin with a single 24" length of 20-gauge wire and use the tall stamen component rather than the button stack as suggested above.

Cluster many small flowers together into hyacinths or delphiniums.

Give leaves body by stitching wire supports through the centers.

Make tall stamens.

» *Incorporate other materials into your flowers.* Decorative paper, leather scraps, bottle caps, brightly colored candy wrappers, and other sorts of fabric can add an element of enchantment.

» *Make a garland of flowers.* These are easiest to make like an actual daisy chain. Make the first flower with a looped stem. The second flower stem hooks into that loop, the third flower hooks into the loop of the second flower stem, and so on.

» *Change the scale of the flowers,* making them smaller with finer wire and smaller bits of fabric. Larger flowers can be quite complicated, requiring strong wire armature to keep the petals from looking wilted, but they can be amazing in super-huge size for parades or fairy parties.

Incorporate other materials into your flowers.

Add leaves to your stems.

HOLLY AND POINSETTIAS

In this case, the only difference between holly and poinsettias is the color of the fabric used. Holly is any sort of green. Poinsettias are white, ivory, scarlet, mulberry, or soft light pink — the colors of natural poinsettias. I use these to add texture and cheer to the Home-for-the-Holidays Wreath on pages 164–168. They are also festive in bunches with stems added for holiday decorating.

you will need

» Felted wool scraps in colors of your choice (see suggestions above)
» Sharp fabric scissors
» A small hand-sewing needle
» Regular sewing thread to match the colors of felt
» A handful of buttons

optional

» Ruler
» 20-gauge galvanized steel wire
» Wire cutters
» Green seam binding or other long, narrow, lightweight green ribbon or fabric strip
» Cordless drill
» White craft glue

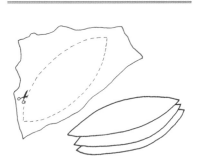

SAMPLE CUTTING LAYOUT

PREPARING YOUR MATERIALS

1. Cut three leaf-shaped pieces from the scraps you have selected for each holly and poinsettia. I like to use three different fabrics here.

2. For each optional stem, cut a 24" length of 20-gauge wire and bend it in half, making the ends even. Repeat for as many stems as desired, and set aside.

CONSTRUCTING THE HOLLY AND POINSETTIA

3. Thread your needle with about 2 yards of thread and knot the two ends together. With a small running stitch, sew across the widest part of one of your leaf shapes. Pull to gather. Secure gather in place by tacking the outside edges together on the back side.

4. With thread still connected, repeat with a second leaf shape. This time tack the gather in place by stitching it to the first leaf shape. The second leaf placement conceals the sewing in the first leaf.

5. The third leaf shape joins the first two the same way, gathered across the middle and sewn in place to make a six-pointed flowerlike shape.

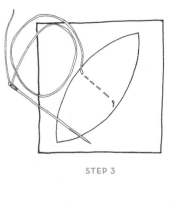

STEP 3

→

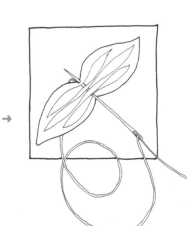

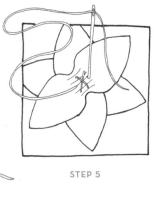

STEP 5

6. Sew on a group of three to six buttons over the center. I use red for holly and white, red, or green for poinsettias. They look best when all the buttons are different styles but the same general color.

ADDING A STEM

7. Beginning at the center top of the flower, poke the wire ends down through all layers of the poinsettia, about ½" apart.

8. Cut a 16" length of lightweight green seam binding, ribbon, or other strip of fabric (I have even used green tissue paper). Fold the end over about 1" and poke one of the wires through both layers of ribbon.

9. Even the ends of the wire with wire cutters, if necessary, and twist together the two ends of the wire either by hand, or by inserting the ends into an electric drill with bit removed. Tighten drill closed around the wires. While holding the flower tightly against the fold in the wire with one hand, gently spin the wires to twist. Be careful not to over twist.

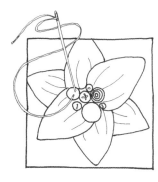

STEP 6

STEP 7

STEP 8

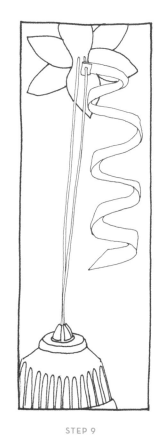

STEP 9

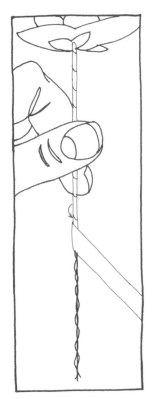

STEP 10

10. Wrap the wire stem with the strip of green fabric fastened in the wire twist: Hold the flat ribbon, angled toward the bottom of the stem, between your thumb and forefinger. Spin the wire with your other hand and let the ribbon pull through your fingers with a little tension. Move along the stem to cover the length with an inch or two of green ribbon to spare.

11. When you get to the bottom, fold the ribbon back onto the stem while continuing to spin the stem in the same direction. When the ribbon is too small to hold onto, put a little dab of white glue on the inside of the ribbon end and press it down smoothly.

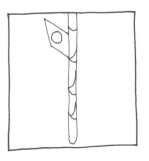

STEP 11

BABY BOOTIES

Here's a project for your larger scraps of extrafelty cloth. (They're pretty slippery on the floor, making them best for kids too small to walk.) Adjust the pattern shapes shown to fit the foot you wish to cover. Sew the back heel seams first, then sew around the circumference of the sole to the shoe top with a running stitch. Make tiny slits for buttonholes in the top ankle bands, and sew buttons to the bottom ankle bands. The buttonholes should be tight going over the button.

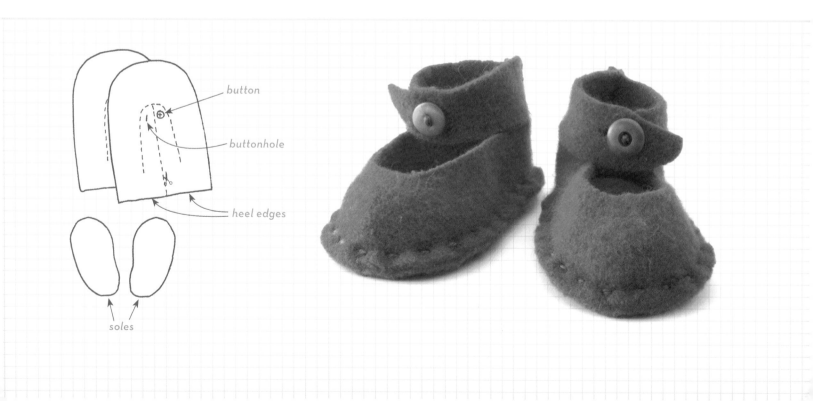

HOME-FOR-THE-HOLIDAYS
WREATH

There are lovely aspects of the holiday season to focus on, one of them being the idea of handmade. Handmade gifts, decorations, and food enhance any experience, and time shared preparing is memorable, empowering, and appreciated. This handmade wreath speaks to that ideal. See it as an inspiration to reduce consumption around these festive occasions and to use what you have to make something to share or to give.

While sewing skills are not in high demand here, you will need a fair amount of upper-body strength for the tying process.

you will need

» About 5 pounds felted wool sweater scraps left-over from other projects
» Sharp fabric scissors or a rotary cutter and pad
» 2 yards extra strong no-stretch twine (baling twine works great)
» A weaving needle that you can thread the baling twine through
» Small spring-loaded pliers

» Work gloves
» A size 14 yarn darner needle
» 2 yards embroidery floss or similar cotton sewing yarn
» A small metal ring designed to hold keys
» Small piece of ribbon or colored tape
» Felted Holly or Poinsettia (see pages 158–162) *or* decorative bow for finished wreath

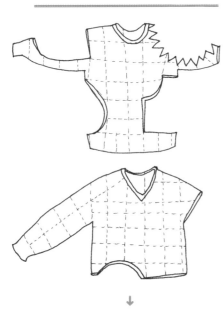

SAMPLE CUTTING LAYOUT

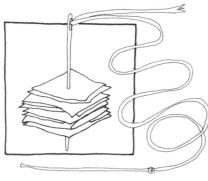

STEP 4

PREPARING YOUR MATERIALS

1. Cut the felted wool material you have gathered into 4" squares. This cut material can be loosely described as squares; it is nice to spice up the look and texture of the finished wreath with occasional oddly shaped bits and pieces. Think about each cut piece having about the same area as a 4" square.

   To avoid pools or blocks of color and make a randomly colored wreath, it is important to cut all the material you will need before you move on to the next step. Put your cut pieces into a laundry basket or bin as you cut. Once you are finished with the cutting process, toss the pieces to ensure a random mix of color throughout.

CONSTRUCTING THE WREATH

2. Place the cut squares in stacks 3" to 4" high; I fold any long skinny ones in half.

3. Thread your large weaving needle with a 2-yard length of baling twine. Make a large double overhand knot about 8" from the end.

4. With your threaded needle, poke through the center of one stack of felted squares, checking to be sure you have pierced each layer as you pick it up. Continue to thread all the stacks of cut goods onto the twine, one after the other, pulling them to the knot as you go. This process is easier with the aid of the pliers. Hold the needle firmly with the pliers. With your other hand, tug the cut goods over the needle and down to meet the knot. Be sure the pieces are laying flat next to each other without being bunched up, adding bulk that will loosen later.

5. Continue to pack the bits tightly together until you have threaded a 42" long "caterpillar" on your baling twine. (I measure this when I am not pushing the pieces down and they are not under pressure.)

6. Wear your work gloves to tie the two ends of the twine in a very strong, nonslip knot. Do this sitting on the floor with the twine between the toes like a flip-flop. Push the fabric away with your feet while pulling the twine tight and trying like hell to knot it well. A loose knot makes a droopy wreath. Use a square knot with an extra go 'round.

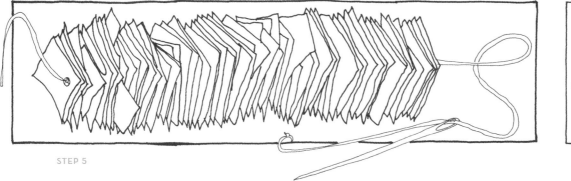

STEP 5

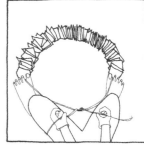

STEP 6

knotting know-how

There are a few things to know about knots and wreaths:

* *It is hard to undo a loose knot and tie it over again.*
* *If you get fabric entangled in the knot, it will loosen more easily.*

* *If you practice tying the knot with the same twine before you make the wreath, it will help you know what you are doing when time is of the essence.*
* *Plan on redoing this step a time or two before you get your desired finish — it is really easy to do it wrong.*

CRISPINA'S
DESIGN NOTES

This project is a great way to use up a lot of fabric scraps. We began making holiday wreaths in an assorted mix of colors from all the leftover wool scraps of my company's wholesale production process. These were an epiphany in our wholesale company's history because they closed the scrap generation-gap by creating a demand for all the leftover material we were not using. There was actually a time when we were making scraps just to fill orders for these!

FINISHING THE WREATH

7. Decide which side is the front. Thread the needle with the embroidery floss, knot both ends together, and attach the key ring to the wreath back with very deep, strong stitches. The ring will be used to hang the wreath, and it looks nicest if it cannot be seen from the front. Mark the ring with a piece of brightly colored tape or ribbon so it is easy to find later.

8. Once you have the base complete, embellish it with a felted Holly sprig (or two) and/or Poinsettias (see pages 158–162). Pay attention to the wreath's orientation, being sure you know where the top is.

9. A wide bow is a nice, traditional holiday addition. Use ribbon or cut a wide strip of pretty cloth from something used and try that. You might have to piece it together to make it long enough. Starch will help it stand crisply.

STEP 7

STEP 9

WREATH VARIATION

»   *Use lighter weight fabrics in pastels* or summery tones or a mix of fabric textures. Play around with the idea and see what you develop.

STOCKINGS

Holiday stockings are time-honored keepsakes that are best when handmade. Here are just a few ideas of ways to use scraps from other projects to make your family's holidays even more meaningful. Embroidery across the top cuff can also be added to personalize and embellish each stocking.

TIME REQUIRED **2 HOURS** *to get going*
and then **10 MINUTES** *per Bobble*

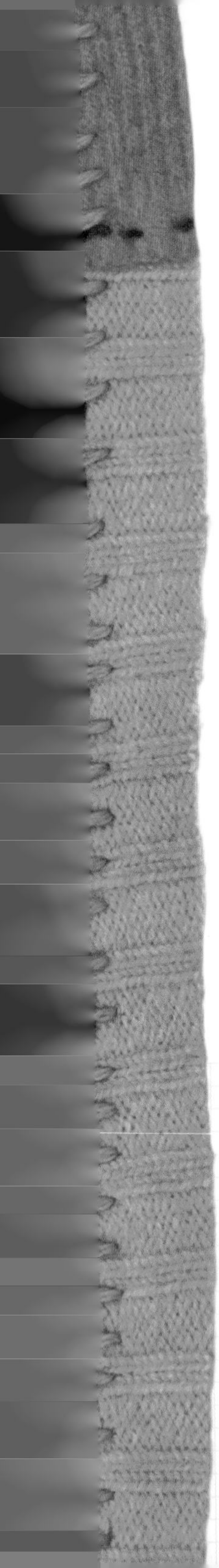

BOBBLES

In general, I warn against using open and loosely knit sweaters for the projects in this book. However, here is the one project that's great for loose knits and they don't have to feel felted at all. The giant holes in the loose knits make them quite easy to sew through when rolled into a 2" or 3" ball. You definitely don't need to go buy sweaters for this. Use any loosely knit material you have on hand. Just avoid very dense felt, cotton, or material that has zippers, buttons, or other hard things that might get in the way later.

These Bobbles are lovely en masse, displayed in a big decorative bowl; they also can be used as ornaments on holiday trees or mantelpieces, or strung together to make festive garlands.

you will need

- » Scraps of open-knit sweaters, scarves, and fabric not useful for other projects, cut 2" × 8" (or longer)
- » Scraps of finely knit wool to use for outside colors of Bobbles, cut 2" × 8", or as long as possible
- » Sharp fabric scissors or a rotary cutter and pad
- » Extra-long straight pins
- » A doll needle
- » Persian wool or embroidery floss

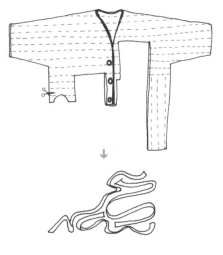

SAMPLE CUTTING LAYOUT

CONSTRUCTING YOUR BOBBLES

1. Make two piles of cut strips: one of the open-knit pieces for the inner core, and one of the stretchier, fine-knit pieces for the outer wrapping layer.

2. Use the open-knit strips to make the core. Starting at one end, roll the strip into a fairly tight ball. If you want to make the Bobble bigger than one strip of cloth will allow, just add another strip by overlapping the end where you left off and carry on. Try to make the Bobble round as you work.

3. When you reach the desired size, poke a pin through the end of the fabric, straight into the ball.

4. Choose the outer strip you would like to use to finish the Bobble. Thin cloth often curls a bit when pulled. Cut one end of the strip you have chosen to a nice sloping point. Gently pull the strip between your two hands to see if the cloth has a natural curl. If so, allow the fabric to curl the same direction as the ball curves (this usually means the wrong side of the fabric will face out).

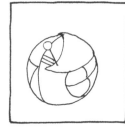
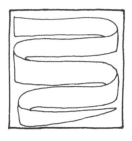

STEP 2   STEP 3   STEP 4

5. Remove the pin from the core and overlap the end of the core fabric with the nonpointed beginning of outer wrapping strip. When wrapping the Bobble, work with the curl rather than against it, even if it means showing the wrong side of the cloth on the outside of the Bobble. As you go, hold the width of the strip between your index and middle fingers and gently pull as you wrap to get a nice tight finish.

STEP 5

6. Once the entire core has been covered, you are finished wrapping. Pin the pointed end of the strip in place by poking a pin straight into the core.

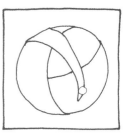

STEP 6

7. Thread a doll needle with a length of yarn about 1½ yards long in a color you like with the color of your Bobble. Knot one end of the yarn.

8. Begin sewing by poking by your needle into the backside of the pointy end of the last strip. As you begin to wrap the yarn, you will conceal the knot with the point of the last strip. Wrap the yarn around the middle of the Bobble (like the equator). Hold your thumb on the "North Pole" (the starting point) and your middle finger on the "South Pole." Wrap yarn around again. This time, move to the left a bit, being sure that you are creating a nice neat intersection at both the poles. Continue to wrap the yarn around the Bobble, moving to the left with each rotation, making "spokes" as you go.

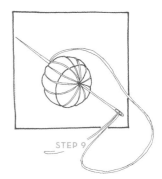

STEP 9

9. When you have evenly spaced spokes around the circumference of the Bobble, gather all the yarns at one of the poles together with your needle and sew straight through the center of the Bobble, coming out at the opposite end. Again, tidy the intersection with your needle and stitch straight back down through the core of the Bobble, emerging at the first pole. Snip off the yarn now, or, if you would like to make a hanger for the Bobble, continue to the next step.

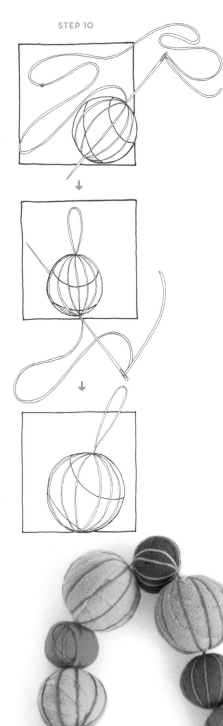

STEP 10

10. To hang the Bobble, make a nice big knot about 8" from the surface of the Bobble on your sewing yarn. Stitch straight down into the bobble, emerging at the opposite pole.

Pull yarn down to the knot. Poke your needle back through the core of the Bobble, exiting on one side. Snip off excess yarn close to the surface of the Bobble.

BOBBLE VARIATIONS

» *Use color for different effects.* Brightly colored ones evoke a winter holiday spirit while all-neutral Bobbles might have a more year-round appeal. A pastel palette would be a lovely decoration for a baby shower, or in a nursery.

» *Use embroidery floss or metallic string* for sewing to add a different texture.

» *Make a whole bunch of Bobbles* of differing sizes and colors and string them on monofilament (fishing line) end-to-end to make a garland.

» *Use beaded sweaters* for the final wrap layer to add sparkle.

» *Make Bobble hangers from metallic gold thread.* Finish the Bobbles without hangers. Cut 7" to 10" lengths of metallic gold string. Tie the ends of the gold string together in a simple overhand knot. Pull middle of metallic string loop under the hub of the intersection with a crochet hook and slip the knotted end of the metallic string through the loop. Firmly pull the knotted end to make the other end flush with the surface of the Bobble.

String the bobbles together to make a garland.

Page numbers in *italics* refer to photographs.

INDEX

OTHER STOREY TITLES YOU WILL ENJOY

Colorful Stitchery, by Kristin Nicholas.
Dozens of embroidery projects to embellish and enhance any home.
208 pages. Paper. ISBN 978-1-58017-611-8.

Felt It!, by Maggie Pace.
Hats, shawls, belts, bags, home accessories — the perfect introduction
to the magic of knitted felt, for all levels of knitters.
152 pages. Paper. ISBN 978-1-58017-635-4.

Making Rag Rugs, by Clare Hubbard.
Beautiful, original designs from a variety of talented rug designers,
explained in clear step-by-step instructions.
80 pages. Paper. ISBN 978-1-58017-455-8.

Sew What! Bags, by Lexie Barnes.
Totes, messenger bags, drawstring sacks, and handbags — 18 pattern-free
projects that can be customized into all shapes and sizes.
152 pages. Hardcover with concealed wire-o. ISBN 978-1-60342-092-1.

Sew What! Skirts, by Francesca DenHartog & Carole Ann Camp.
A fast, straightforward method to sewing a variety of inspired skirts that
fit your body perfectly, without relying on store-bought patterns.
128 pages. Hardcover with concealed wire-o. ISBN 978-1-58017-625-5.

These and other books from Storey Publishing are available
wherever quality books are sold or by calling 1-800-441-5700.
Visit us at www.storey.com.